Valentine Love

PAM KELLY

VALENTINE LOVE

This book is a work of fiction. Names, characters, businesses, organizations, places, events, and incidents either are the product of the author's research, or imagination, or are used fictitiously. Any resemblance to actual persons, living or dead, or events, is entirely coincidental.

Copyright © 2022 by Pamela F. Kelly

All rights reserved. The reproduction, transmission, or utilization of this work, in whole or in part, in any form by electronic, mechanical, or other means, now known or hereafter invented, including xerography, photocopying, or recording, or in any information storage or retrieval system, except brief quotes used in reviews, is forbidden without written permission. For permission, please contact Pamela F. Kelly: Pam@PamelaFKelly.com

ISBN: 978-0-9801502-5-4 (paperback)

ISBN: 978-0-9801502-6-1 (ebook)

Texas Divorce Law Consultant:
    Dessiray Cusic (TheCusicLawFirm.com)
Medical Consultant: Sharon Harris, BSN
Editor: Hilda R. Davis, PhD. (HildaRDavis.com)
Beta Readers: Beverly Franklin, Lori Perkins, Kimberly Roy,
    Maurice Walker, Ruby Walker, Dr. Franzetta
    Woodard
Cover Design: Mary Ann Smith (Reedsy.com)

Also by PAM KELLY:

LEAP OF FAITH
A Romance Novel

DEDICATION

To those who have never had a great love
It is never too late to love

To all the women and men who say:
"I'm too old"/ "I'm done with that"/
"I don't think about it anymore"
It is okay to believe in love again

And to those who have loved and
lost and want another
"I have learned not to worry about love;
But to honor its coming with all my heart."
~Alice Walker

"Loving someone liberates the lover as well as the beloved. And that kind of love comes with age."

~Maya Angelou

Chapter One

Jefferson Ware and Valerie Mason both woke up excited that the day would end with them finally being alone together. They met the day before Valentine's Day at Fay's Flower Shop where she worked, and had seen each other since then, but always with other people around them or with them. Today was the day for just the two of them to be together and get to know one another. Jefferson was cooking dinner for her at his house. She was eager to see him in his personal space.

Jefferson spent the morning cleaning his home and putting fresh linen on the bed (just in case), then went grocery shopping. The menu was simple: stuffed baked pork chops, sautéed vegetables, a salad, and dinner rolls with herb butter. For dessert, he made a key lime pie, her favorite she said when they had lunch on Saturday, even though she had not ordered it.

He was making every effort to impress her, and had followed his dad's sage advice to make a grand gesture when he wanted to secure a woman's attention. He had already made two grand gestures and received confirmation that she was impressed each time. He wanted a special ladylove, and knew in his heart that Valerie was the one. The dinner was to "seal the deal" – get Valerie to say she was interested in spending more time with him. If everything worked out as he hoped, they would soon be in an exclusive relationship.

For some people it might seem to be too soon to want to be exclusive. But Jefferson was a man of a certain age who had plenty of experience with women to know when the right one came along. He was decisive and determined to enjoy life with someone special. Valerie was that someone.

Promptly at five, Jefferson's doorbell rang. He danced to the door, opening it with a grin on his face and a special greeting. "Welcome home my Valentine Love," he said pointedly. His eyes took in the colorful midi dress, sweater, and knee-high boots she wore and he commented, "I don't know how you do it, but you look more beautiful and sexy every time I see you."

Valerie had a grin on her face too. She was glad that she had dressed to show her feminine, bohemian side and appreciated that he noticed. The other times they had seen each other she had on pants.

She replied in kind, "Thank you, it's good to be here. And you look mighty handsome yourself." Jefferson wore a short sleeved no collar shirt and jeans with shoes and no socks. To Valerie, his look was casual yet very sexy. The evening was off to a great start.

She had brought a vase filled with Hydrangeas for this visit, not knowing if he had a favorite flower. She wanted to leave a little bit of herself, her favorite flower, in his house. He was surprised, and immediately set the flowers on the entry table and gave her a hug.

She felt good in his arms and smelled wonderful so he took his time before releasing her. She was enjoying him too so she did not pull away. Reluctantly, he let her go, picked up the flowers, and headed to the kitchen, placing the flowers on the table where they were going to eat.

"Really nice house Jefferson." Valerie was impressed as she followed him. It was a ranch house or flat as they call it in Houston, with large rooms and wood floors. He took her on a tour, back through the family room to his bedroom and two guest bedrooms, then a huge den where he said they had family Game Day, watching sports or playing games. The color scheme was blue, purple, and white with touches of silver. Each room had colorful rugs, and blankets or throws on the beds and near the seating, making you want to snuggle up to read a book, watch television, or take a nap.

There were candles burning in the family room and den. The scents were fresh and lush. She immediately felt like she was at home and was even more excited to get to know this very confident man.

Jefferson sat her on the banquette side of the extra tall table set he built to accommodate the long legs on his six foot three frame, giving her a full view of the kitchen. Pausing to make sure she was settled and had water, he then leaned over to press his lips softly on hers.

"Mmm. Thank you! Wait. No toothpick today?" Valerie was teasing him because each time she had seen him over the weekend he had one in his mouth.

"No. I told you it was a placeholder to keep my tongue busy until I could kiss you. Now that you are here…" He decided not to wait any longer to get what he wanted from the first day he saw her. He held her face and his tongue slowly licked her lips, nudging them apart. He slid his tongue in and played with hers for a while. His tongue was long and commanded her attention and response.

They both moaned at the same time and he pulled her to the edge of the seat so she would be close to his body. They spent the next five minutes tasting and sucking each other's tongue, kissing cheeks, and licking lips. The longer they kissed, the tighter they held each other. Neither wanted to stop. They did so only when his cell phone rang. He did not answer it.

They looked at each other, both knowing that the hugging and kissing stoked the desire they had been feeling from the first day they met. It was confirmation that something special was happening between them.

Chapter Two

The rattling of a pot on the stove reminded them of dinner so Jefferson went back to his preparations.

"The food smells delicious. What can I do to help?" She enjoyed watching him operate, going from the stove to the sink to the fridge like a professional chef.

"You can help me by sitting your beautiful self at the table and talk to me. I just want to look at you while I finish up. So, how was your day?"

"It was good. Nice and quiet again at work since Valentine's Day is over. I was able to upload the sales receipts quickly and leave."

"So you're an accountant?" He paused to stand by her and listen to her answer. Watching her mouth move made it hard to concentrate on what she was saying. He wanted to kiss her again and not just a quick press on the lips.

"I'm not an accountant actually. My parents were both math instructors so numbers and technology came easily for my older sister, Stephanie and me. She became a techie in Silicon Valley and now does product design for Google. I majored in math then became a math teacher in a couple of high schools here and at Texas Southern University.

"A few years ago, I took classes the IRS offered on taxes and software so I could help Fay on weekends or when I was on break. With my divorce settlement, I retired from teaching. I work at the flower shop during the week now instead of weekends, four hours on Mondays and Thursdays. In addition to processing the receipts, I prepare quarterly reports so that she is ready for tax season. I also take orders on holidays, as you know." She smiled.

She was giving him details on her life while she noticed how good he smelled, standing so close. She licked her lips, anticipating more kissing to come but probably not until after dinner.

"Tell me more. Where you grew up. About your parents. How long were you married? You just have one child, your daughter?" She had not talked about herself on their brief nightly calls, letting him lead the conversations. He always kept them focused on letting her know that he was interested and wanted to schedule a date. He kept the calls short to be considerate of her need to rest up for work.

"Grew up here in Houston in a house not far from Rice University. My parents met on a blind date during graduate school, dated for about three years then got married. They both taught at the college level, him for Rice, her for the University of Houston. Steph came along two years later, then me two years after that.

"They died a few years ago. He had Alzheimer's. She took care of him at home. Right after he died, she was diagnosed with breast cancer. It was aggressive and took her quickly." Valerie paused for a drink of water, not used to talking about herself and her family in such detail. It had been a while since anyone asked. It was okay though because she wanted him to know about her.

"I'm sorry," he said quietly. "But I still want to know about you. Keep going."

"I married Vincent when I was in my early thirties. We just have the one daughter. Her name is Veronica but we call her Nikki." She was smiling again, clearly happy to talk about her.

"Your family has a thing for the letter "V" huh?" Jefferson thought it was funny.

"You don't know the half of it." Valerie informed him, "Vincent has a brother, Victor, and a sister, Viveca. It's a Mason thing." They both laughed.

"My ex is President of Operations at Unity Bank. He became a cliché, sleeping with one of his managers. I don't share." She paused and took another sip of water.

He responded with compassion. "Okay. Good to know. I hope I didn't make you sad. I just wanted to know something about you." He walked over to the table, put his arms around her, and hugged her.

"I'm good, thanks. It was tough knowing someone could come between us after we had been married for so long. Both of us were looking forward to retiring young and having a grand time traveling. The joke was on me."

Jefferson felt the conversation needed to shift to something more positive and fun and was glad that dinner was finally ready. He plated their food then they said grace and began to eat. The food was delicious and they both ate slowly, savoring each bite. Jefferson decided to share information about his family while they enjoyed it.

"I have just one sibling also. My sister Jeannette lives about ten minutes away. Her son, Steven, and Steven's son Jason were the ones at the flower shop with me on Thursday. They live around the corner from her. I took financial care of Jeannette when Steven's dad died so she could get her college degree and a good job to take care of herself and her son. She has worked in research for a few different oil companies over the years since graduating and is doing quite well. Steven also works for an oil company, as an engineer.

"Our parents died a few years ago after being married for almost seventy years. Mom died first and I guess dad missed her so he died not even six months later.

"I was married once myself. Young, fresh out of the Air Force. My wife was headed to medical school. The agreement was that I would put her through school and pay all the bills then she would do the same for me while I attended engineering school.

"Talk about the joke being on you with plans to travel with your husband? The joke was on me with Alicia. The day before she got her medical degree, I was served with divorce papers and told not to attend the graduation ceremony. All of a sudden, I was not good enough for her and her new doctor friends."

Valerie looked at him to see if he was angry or bitter but he seemed very matter of fact about the whole situation. Maybe because it was so long ago.

They cleaned the kitchen together, singing along with the old R&B songs streaming on Alexa and doing some of the dance moves from back in the day. When they stopped dancing, she leaned against the island, watching him put the leftovers in the refrigerator.

"I really enjoyed dinner. You are a great cook. Thank you." She was not just being polite.

He talked as he worked. "Thank you. My momma was a great cook and she believed that her kids needed to know how to cook as well. My cabinets and fridge are fully stocked, and I have cooked some of everything, from soups to desserts. It came in handy through the years since I have lived the single life for so long. I'm glad you enjoyed it."

He closed the refrigerator door then slowly walked over to the island, standing very close in her personal space. "Truthfully though, this is how you can thank me," he said quietly as he pulled her into his arms for another kiss, this one slow and sensual. They paused to hold each other for another moment. Finally, he took her hand and led her to the den where he put on some soft music. They sat down, immediately leaning toward each other to kiss some more.

Chapter Three

The sofa was large and extra deep. Like the kitchen table, it was designed to accommodate his long legs. If you took the thick pillows off the back, it was almost the width of a full size bed. He laid her down with her head on the pillow on the armrest and took off her boots, rubbing her legs, then opening them so he could lay between them on top of her. Immediately she could feel how hard he was. He was rubbing her breasts and arms, kissing her cheeks and neck and back up to her mouth again. She smelled and tasted so good, he could not get enough of her.

She was rubbing his back and arms and shoulders, trying to get as close to him as possible. They were happy to hold one another and kiss slowly, settling back to do so for the rest of the evening. Both were hungry for closeness, especially in the excitement of a new relationship.

All of a sudden, the doorbell rings and someone is banging hard on the front door. Jefferson and Valerie stopped quickly and sat up, adjusting their clothes.

"Someone had better be dead," he muttered, furious that they were interrupted.

He walked out of the room to the front door. Valerie turned off the music.

"Who is it?" he yelled. "And why are you banging on my door like that? Are you crazy?"

When he snatched the door open, he was surprised and pissed. Helen was just about to bang again and he grabbed her hand. She was a lady he had been having lunch with on a regular basis for a couple of months but stopped seeing recently because he knew the friendship was not going to lead to a more personal relationship. She was starting to hint that she wanted more and since he didn't, he told her at their last lunch that he would not be seeing her anymore.

"What are you doing here? What do you want?" She tried to step inside but he stood in her way, making it clear that she was not welcome and would not be going into the house.

She sounded like she had been drinking. "Why don't you answer my calls? I've been calling you for two days!"

"What do you want Helen? And make it quick. I'm busy."

"Talk to me Jeff. Why didn't you go to the wedding with me this weekend? I was hoping we could get past this so-called "friendship" and kiss or have sex or something. Don't you find me attractive? Sexy?"

"Where is this coming from Helen? I told you from the beginning that we were just friends. When I told you I would not go to the wedding with you, I told you that things had not changed for me, and in fact, I would not be seeing you anymore. I never wanted our hanging out to give you the wrong signal. I thought I was clear." He was trying to be kind but was obviously agitated.

"Yes, but I was just hoping if we went away together that would change. Are you gay or something? You don't like women?" She was desperate for answers so she wouldn't feel so bad.

"No Helen, I'm not gay. I thought you were nice and fun so we hung out. I'm just not interested in you romantically and thought I was keeping things honest, not getting too personal. I see being nice was a mistake. You have to go."

Just as she turned to leave, he asked her, "How did you get my address anyway?" He knew he had never given it to her and the friend who introduced them knew Jefferson liked to keep his home life private. He liked to go to the woman's house he was dating so he could leave when he got ready.

"I took down your license plate number. I have friends at the DMV. You never invited me over and I wondered why. What are you hiding? You said you were not married so I figured you had something else going on. You were so secretive," she muttered, figuring she had nothing to lose by telling him.

"I'm not hiding anything. I just like my privacy. Don't come back here anymore. And lose my number. I don't like this kind of noise and craziness." His voice had turned cold and harsh.

He nudged her to get off the porch then slammed the door and watched her drive away before heading back to the den. Valerie could hear him muttering, "Damn, damn, damn."

He walked back into the den to find Valerie with her boots on, purse hanging off her shoulder, and standing by the sofa, waiting for him to come back so she could leave. She looked at him sympathetically when he walked into the room.

"I think I should go. It looks like you have some business that doesn't include me." She talked softly, but was firm in her tone.

He didn't say a word, but looked in her eyes as he took the purse strap off her shoulder and laid the purse on the table, then held her in his arms. "I'm sorry about that. This is not how I saw this evening playing out. Please don't go."

He could feel her body was stiff, nothing like her softness when they were kissing, so he kept his arms around her.

"I told you about Helen the day I met you. I hope you heard the conversation just now so you know I didn't lie about my relationship with her. Just friends. No kissing. No sex. I have not answered her calls because I knew about three weeks or so ago it was time to stop the friendship and told her that." His voice was quiet and tender. His hold on her remained tight.

"I want to get to know you Valerie, and I'm going to hold on to you until you really hear me. I know you are upset and I don't blame you. But please try to relax."

She was tall, even in flat-heeled boots, so her face was near his shoulder. He rested his lips on her forehead. They stood that way for several minutes before he began to feel the tension start to leave her body. Finally, she pushed him away and asked if they could sit. They did, but she still could not relax completely. They sat side by side, both facing the television.

He turned toward her, apologizing profusely. "I am really sorry. This is why I never have women over here. Things get too familiar too fast and they are hard to pull back. You are here because I have a feeling you are different and I hope that we are going to be together for a long time. Please don't let the interruption spoil an otherwise perfect evening."

Neither of them said anything for the next few minutes. Both were thinking.

She did hear the conversation between Helen and Jefferson. While it confirmed that they were not in an intimate relationship, it was still unsettling for her to, even unknowingly, help cause heartbreak to another woman. On the other hand, the earlier part of the evening -- dinner, dancing, cleaning the kitchen together, and kissing, oh the kissing -- had confirmed that she liked him a lot and wanted more. Why should she give him up when she did not break them up?

Jefferson was angry with himself for going out with Helen too long, but was more nervous that Valerie would leave and not give him another chance. He didn't know her well enough to know what to do to keep her from being upset with him, or what she would do when she was upset. He decided to ask if she would watch a movie with him. She nodded her head yes.

They sat facing the television, and he positioned the pillows so they could lean back and watch a comedy, something to lighten the mood.

Before long they were both asleep, which was good to Jefferson because he wanted her to spend the night anyway.

After about an hour, he woke up to turn the television off, take her boots back off, and reposition them on the sofa. He threw the pillows from the back of the sofa on to the floor so they had more room, then he slowly turned her body so that she was stretched out and would be more comfortable. He laid down next to her and put his arm around her. Just before he fell back to sleep he said the line he ended their calls with each night: "Dream of us."

She woke up in the middle of the night and realized they were stretched out on the sofa together and he had his arm around her. Her head was on his chest. She decided she liked lying with him and being wrapped in his arms so she sighed, snuggled closer, and went back to sleep.

He felt her move when she woke up and he woke up too but did not open his eyes or say anything. When he felt her get more comfortable and relax into sleep, he smiled and went back to sleep.

Chapter Four

Valerie woke up the next morning alone in the den. She could smell coffee brewing and heard doors opening and closing in the kitchen. She could also hear Jefferson on the phone.

She took a moment to assess their evening together and affirm in her mind that she had a good time with Jefferson, even with Helen's visit interrupting them. Dinner was great, he was nice to talk to, and it felt really good to sleep with a man again, even if it was on a sofa instead of in a bed. She got excited thinking about the next time they would be together and whether a bed would be involved. Her thoughts made her body grow warm.

As she looked around the den, she noticed a set of towels on the coffee table along with a new toothbrush, toothpaste, and a small bottle of mouthwash. Valerie chuckled to herself thinking that Jefferson was very prepared for a man who didn't have ladies at his house. It was okay. She appreciated his thoughtfulness and was just glad to be able to freshen up before seeing him.

She walked into the kitchen with her purse, ready to go home. He was sitting at the table going over some papers but looked up and gave her a contemplative look, trying to figure out her mood.

"Good morning," they both said it at the same time, in somber voices.

She got a bottle of water out of the fridge and when she turned around, he had turned from the table to face her and held his arms open for her to come to him. She put her purse and bottle on the table and walked over to him, standing between his legs, placing her hands on his thighs. He pulled her up close so he could whisper in her ear. "I enjoyed sleeping with you and waking up with you here this morning. What do I need to do to make that happen every day?" He started rubbing her back.

She wasn't sure he was serious but liked the idea even though she knew it was way too soon for that. She had to give him credit, however, for being bold and putting his desire for her out there.

"Jeff," was all she could say softly in response in his ear.

If there was such thing as an eargasm, he had one every time she whispered his name in his ear. It felt like she had put her hand down his pants and was stroking him. It happened every night when they talked on the phone and he had to reposition himself in the bed or chair. This time she could see his facial expression as he reacted to her voice and her breath on his ear. She smiled to herself, glad to know that he liked her voice like that.

She felt movement under her hand and looked down, feeling him grow big and hard. She looked up at him and started rubbing his thigh while asking,

"You want me here every day? You sure about that? You think you could handle that?"

He grabbed her hand to stop the movement and the sensation that was rapidly spreading throughout his body.

"You keep doing that and I will handcuff you to the bed. Neither one of us will leave here today," he whispered in her ear. He wanted to see how far he could go with the sexy banter.

She gave him a saucy response. "Handcuffs, huh? Okay. And what other toys and tricks do you have for us to play with?" She smiled to let him see that she could give as good as he did.

"Oh, I can think of a few," he said with a wink.

They both laughed and she turned her back to him to walk away but he put his arm around her to stop her. She leaned back on him and listened as he began explaining the papers on the table, his schedule for the week.

"There are about ten houses that need something every day: a bulb out, toilet problems, they smell gas. Every week it's a different set of houses but similar problems. Today we have to replace a water heater."

"We?" She was curious.

"Me and Ron. He started as an apprentice but now works full time." While he was answering, he wrapped his hands around her breasts, rubbing them until her nipples stood at attention.

"Are these for me?" He inquired in her ear while squeezing her nipples gently then kissing her ear and neck.

She was enjoying the feeling but moved his hands, telling him to, "Stop being a distraction.

"I need to go home and you need to go to work so don't start what you have no time to finish." Her face was flushed. She knew where they were heading. Was she being too loose? Too eager? She decided she didn't care. She wanted what she wanted and usually got it. Most often, it was clothes, shoes, or a trip. Now it was a man. This man.

Today she wanted him and he wanted her. It was just a matter of time before they were "together" and she was not going to worry about what came afterwards.

He asked if he could fix her breakfast before she headed out. Declining the offer, she asked for a raincheck. He was happy to hear that she was thinking that they would likely have another morning together and agreed. She gathered her purse and water to leave.

He stood up, preparing to walk her to her car, and slid a card across the table with some numbers on it: 0214. Valentine's Day.

"This code will open both the front door as well as the kitchen door if you come through the garage. The number for the alarm company is on the front of the card. If you run into problems and the alarm goes off, call the company. I might not be able to answer if you call me but I am sure they will."

Valerie was taken aback. He was very trusting and she fussed at him for being so. "You are too trusting Jefferson. I could never open my home like that to someone I knew less than a week."

He agreed. "Normally I don't, but I trust you. Besides, what would you do? Take some furniture? I'll buy more. And I can cancel the code remotely. I want you to start making your way in and out of here on your own."

"This still feels odd." She tried to sound casual but it was not working. "I'll come back when you are home. Since you are working today, I'll come back over when we are both off." She turned toward the family room to go out to her car.

He stopped her at the door and looked closely in her face with a very serious expression.

"I meant what I said. I want you here. I enjoy you in a way I haven't enjoyed anyone in a long, long time. And unless I've totally lost my mind, I think you are feeling me too. I know we are still getting to know each other so we will pace ourselves. How about you go home and pack a bag so you can stay here for the rest of the week. Go to work from here and whatever else you do during your days. We will take it a week at a time. How's that?"

The look on her face expressed her surprise at his invitation. She was not sure of what she wanted to say. She was happy, but things were happening very fast. The phrase "be careful what you pray for" ran through her mind.

"So take the card," he continued after she didn't say anything, "and I'll see you tonight. I'll be home at six. I'll call you when I'm on my way to see what I can bring for dinner. If you are coming back later than six, just let me know when you will be getting home so I can look out for you." With that, he kissed her lips with just the tip of his tongue going in her mouth and walked her outside.

"Be safe my Valentine Love, and have a great day. See you tonight." He watched her back out of the driveway and his heart was full.

He knew already he was falling in love with her. Hell, he probably had the "love at first sight" feeling the first day he walked into Fay's Flowers on Thursday and laid eyes on her. He had a few minutes before he had to leave for work so he sat in the kitchen with a second cup of coffee to reflect on the events leading up to today…

It was Thursday, the day before Valentine's Day, and she was taking flower orders at the counter as well as over the phone. When she heard the door chime, she looked up. The electromagnetic energy that passed between them with just a look was so strong you could almost see it, like lightening charging across the floor. He continued staring as he walked slowly yet directly to her, put his hand on hers, and started twirling the pearl ring on her left hand. She tried not to look at him but the force was so strong, she found herself staring at him too and didn't pull her hand away. She had answered all of his questions. Her voice was like velvet rubbing on his ears, a definite erogenous zone.

"Are you married? Valerie is it?" He asked, looking at her nametag.

"Yes, it's Valerie, and no, I'm not married anymore."

"Engaged?" He asked next.

She said no, then asked, with a smile and a little playfulness, "Are you married or engaged?"

"No wife, not engaged," he said smiling, then asked, *"Are you committed to anyone?"*

"What does that mean exactly—"committed"?"

"Are you someone's exclusive partner? Valentine's Love? Friend with benefits?" He said the last part with one eyebrow raised.

"No, no, and definitely not. What about you? Who in your life is looking forward to flowers and you tomorrow? Or maybe even tonight?" She was bold too since he was asking so many questions.

He stopped twirling the ring and just held her hand before responding. He told her about Helen being a friend with no benefits that he had lunch with from time to time then paused to gauge her reaction. She looked away for a moment as if thinking about what he had just said. He didn't wait for her to respond, continuing the litany of questions.

"So, Ms. Valerie, what kind of flowers do you like?"

She responded slowly, "Hydrangea's. White ones," once again looking at him. She seemed magnetized by his steady gaze and he liked that he was having that effect on her.

"Good to know," he nodded, still looking in her eyes. "So will you go out to dinner with me tomorrow and be my Valentine?"

Valerie's blush conveyed that she was flattered and interested, until she said, "I can't. But thanks for the invitation."

Valerie finally stopped staring at Jefferson and pulled her hand back to complete the order for his nephew Steven who had just walked up to the counter with two vases of flowers.

Jefferson asked her one last time, "Are you sure about tomorrow?"

"I'm sure. Thanks." She spoke softly, and her look was of disappointment. His was too.

He left the flower shop thinking of how to make his first grand gesture and found his opportunity to make it happen about an hour later. Passing by the shop on his way home after dropping off Steven and Jason, he could see through the window that Valerie was not at the register taking orders. He quickly pulled over and called the flower shop, speaking with one of the workers, Billy, who was happy to help him.

Jefferson bought all of the white Hydrangeas in the flower shop and asked Billy to make a big presentation to Valerie, including a card that he dictated. Apparently, Billy knew just what to do because when Valerie called him that night he could hear the excitement in her voice as she told him what the team had done and thanked him.

"Billy and Reyna and Fay were lined up in front of the table in the break room where we usually eat and talk. Billy stood in front of the table; Fay and Reyna were behind him standing side by side. They were all smiling.

"When I asked what was going on, Billy walked over, took my arm and said, "Ms. Mason, Happy Valentine's Day."

"Fay and Reyna parted in the middle like the Red Sea and exposed the biggest bouquet of white

Hydrangea's that I have ever seen. They were actually in three large vases but grouped together to look like one huge presentation.

"I couldn't imagine who they were from but to be honest, I was hoping they were from you.

"Then Billy presented the card with a flourish and a deep bend at the waist, saying, "He is so romantic. I need to take lessons from him to step up my game."

"I loved the card." Then she read it to him as if he had not dictated it to Billy: "Valerie. Please call me before you go to bed. No matter what time. We have a lot to talk about and I would love to start the conversation tonight. Jeff."

She confessed, "I couldn't wait to get home and call. I'm very curious about you."

Jefferson had smiled at her reaction, knowing that he had impressed her. "I'm glad to hear that," he responded.

That was the first of their nightly calls. He immediately started a special way of saying goodnight by asking her to "dream of us" so that she would go to sleep with him, and them being together, on her mind.

He executed his second grand gesture the next day, taking lunch to the whole team as a thank you for their help with the flower presentation. It was a good excuse to see Valerie again. She was smiling when he showed up with the big box of soul food dinners, happy to see him too.

On Saturday, he had lunch with Valerie and her best friend who had driven in from Austin, Texas. He thought it went well until Lillian invited him to come with Valerie to her wedding anniversary party in August. Valerie was clearly uncomfortable and would not look at him. He wasn't concerned. It was months away so there was time to work it out.

Monday evening with dinner, "getting to know you" conversation, and the kissing confirmed that he was happy, ready to love her. He had a feeling that Ms. Valerie Mason was happy with him too. If she came back to stay for the week, he would know that he was closer to sealing the deal.

With those thoughts in his head, he left for work with a smile on his face and excitement stirring his body. It was going to be a long day, anticipating whether she would be at his house when he called at five.

Chapter Five

Valerie drove away from Jefferson's house in a daze. Jefferson was right, she was feeling him as she had not felt anyone in a long time, probably since Vincent, her former husband. Maybe not even Vincent. He had been charming, handsome, comfortable, and dependable, all the things you are told to want in a husband.

Jefferson, however, was fire and fun and forceful, living on the edge and pulling you along for the ride, not giving you a chance to catch your breath. Yet also serious with an appreciation for life that few people get to experience or enjoy.

Life was very different now for Valerie than when she was younger or married. No worries about school, work, husband, or baby. Just enjoying herself. This felt like such a fairy-tale. Exciting, fun, carefree. She really wanted to give in to the feelings she was having for Jefferson, get swept up in his energy. But was she ready for staying a week with this new man, or even for a full blown relationship? Was he really being a stalker making things move so quickly? Should she be concerned that he might want something from her?

Morning traffic was still heavy so she had to drive slowly. It gave her time to think and replay the events of their meeting on Thursday, and seeing Jefferson on Friday and Saturday, hoping it would help her find reasons not to go back to his house so soon, or reasons not to stay for a week...

When Jefferson came in to the flower shop with his two nephews, she knew right away that he was a force to be reckoned with. She could feel it in her bones. The energy between them was palpable. Watching him walk his sexy, slow walk to the counter took her breath away. He stared at her, smiling when she looked in his face.

He walked to the counter looking her up and down and smiling as he was enjoying the view. Jefferson had a shaven baldhead, salt and pepper mustache and beard, black irises in up-turned eyes, and very kissable lips. All she could do was grip the counter and wait for the events to unfold. The young man he was with, Steven, who looked to be in his thirties, pointed to the refrigerated section to let Jefferson know that he and the little boy she now knew as Stevens son, Jason, were going to look at the pre-made bouquets. Jefferson remained standing in front of Valerie, putting his hand on top of hers to twirl her ring, waiting for her to say something.

Valerie smiled to herself as she thought of her opening comments. She was trying to sound professional, but light-hearted, fun, not wanting to look too eager...

"Well hello there. This is my lucky day. I get to help three men make some women very happy Valentine's. So are you the one responsible for this line *of handsome men? What kind of flowers would your wife like?"*

"No," Jefferson responded quietly, as he twirled the pearl ring around on her finger. "I am their uncle, Jefferson Ware. And I don't have a wife." Once she looked at him, she was done. Toast. Swept up in his magnetism.

She liked the way he asked if she was single or engaged or committed to anyone, making it clear that he was interested. His voice was raspy, like he was a smoker but he said he never did. It was so sexy to her she could listen to him talk all day.

She had to turn down his invitation to Valentine's Day dinner because she had to work but told him that she was committed to helping Fay for the day at the flower shop, not uninterested. He seemed disappointed but understanding. Then he blew her away with buying all of the white Hydrangeas and having the staff present them to her. Talk about what he called a grand gesture! It was nice to feel wanted again in such a personalized way.

Friday was a busy Valentine's Day and she was taking orders again at the register while Fay, Billy, and Reyna filled them. Jefferson made it a special day by bringing lunch for the staff. He was only there a few short minutes, but they smiled at each other like school kids with their first crush the whole time.

She invited him to eat lunch with her but he turned her down. "I'm good, thanks. I just wanted to see you and wish you a Happy Valentine's Day. Now that I have, I'll let you get back to work." That's when she noticed the toothpick in his mouth. She didn't mention it, thinking that he had just eaten. But there was one in his mouth on Saturday when he met her and her best friend Lillian for lunch at Maggiano's, her favorite Italian restaurant. She and Lillian always ate there when Lillian drove down from Austin. Only this time they had company for lunch.

Honking horns brought Valerie out of her reverie and she realized the light had turned green so she eased off the brake and moved through the intersection. She decided to make a stop at the mall a few blocks away to grab lunch to take home, which reminded her of lunch on Saturday...

Valerie and Lillian arrived at Maggiano's at 12:45pm and waited for Jefferson before being seated. When he walked in, the hair on Valerie's neck and arms stood up. She could feel his presence even though she could not see him. He put his hand on her shoulder and she put her hand on top of his, still not turning around. He whispered in her ear, "You look fabulous and smell delicious. I'll take all of whatever you are serving up for lunch."

She was glad they were being guided to their booth so she could hide her red face. It had been a long time since she had blushed. She knew Jefferson saw that her work uniform covered up a curvy, shapely body-- full breasts, a small waist, and nice sized hips. Her long natural salt and pepper hair was loose and wild that day, like a lion's mane. Men especially liked it like that and from the way Jefferson kept looking at her head and smiling throughout lunch, he was no exception.

Valerie was sliding to the middle of the booth when Jefferson asked, "Where are you going? Don't go so far away." She stopped and he slid in close to her.

Lillian sat across from Jefferson and introductions were made. He expressed his joy at the invitation to lunch. "I really appreciate being able to spend time with you ladies. I get to know so much more about Ms. Valerie and get to know her best friend in the process. That's what I call a win-win."

The conversation flowed freely. Jefferson was clearly comfortable with them and Lillian was enjoying the interplay between Jefferson and her best friend. Jefferson made it a point to engage Lillian in conversation to know about her and her husband. He was attentive to her when she talked but every chance he got, he was looking at Valerie, giving her the same look as the first day they met: direct, long, and clearly only for her. He had a toothpick in his mouth again so she asked why since they had just sat down to eat.

He responded softly in her ear, "It's a placeholder. I want to kiss you but it's not time yet so I use the toothpick to keep my tongue busy."

She looked at his mouth and he slid his tongue out to lick his lips and move the toothpick from the left side of his mouth to the right side. Then she looked in his eyes. They smiled at each other and she shook her head and rolled her eyes, as if she couldn't believe he would say and do that.

"What? Too much information? Too direct for you?" He smiled at her then turned his head to focus on what Lillian was saying.

Lillian shook her head too. She didn't hear what he said, but she could feel the heat waves rolling off of them the whole time. She already knew there was some serious chemistry between them. She liked him, and she liked him for her friend. He was a nice looking, confident man who didn't seem to have an agenda. Seasoned and feisty, just enjoying life. He could give Valerie the fun and love she wanted and needed.

Lunch was ordered and served. While Lillian ate a salmon salad, Valerie shared some of her Fettuccine Alfredo with Jefferson in exchange for a taste of his Spaghetti and Meatball. It felt natural to share food with each other.

They discovered during the conversation that Jefferson was five years younger than Lillian and Valerie. Jefferson leaned to the right away from Valerie, looking her up and down in that "I see you" way that men sometimes do, then stretched his arm across the back of the booth to touch her shoulder. His comment was an old school joke: "Look at you Ms. Valerie, robbing my cradle."

He paused to look her up and down again then said, "Don't worry. I'm alright with that." He gave a sly smile and Valerie and Lillian laughed. They both enjoyed his sense of humor.

Valerie made the quick stop for her food and headed home. She remembered the one sour note of the lunch with Lillian and Jefferson…

Everything was going well until Lillian invited Jefferson to her thirty-fifth wedding anniversary party. When Jefferson looked at Valerie to get her approval, she would not look at him, making a big deal of looking in her purse. He looked back at Lillian and said sadly, "Looks like Ms. Valerie might have already made other plans. But thanks anyway." He then whispered to

Valerie, "I don't want to be anywhere you don't want me. It's okay."

Jefferson talked more with Lillian but Valerie was quiet. Embarrassed. Lunch ended pleasantly, but Valerie was still uncomfortable. Jefferson was kind as he prepared to leave. "Thank you for a great time ladies. It has been nice getting to know you both. Safe travels back to Austin Ms. Lillian."

Lillian invited him to hang out with them for the rest of the day. They were going to an art fair. He declined.

"No thanks. I think I need to give Ms. Valerie some space. Besides, you two don't have much time to be together if you're leaving tomorrow. Have fun. Ms. Valerie, will you call me before you go to sleep tonight so that I can say goodnight? Unless you are out and about until the wee hours. If you are, I will understand." Valerie nodded her head yes.

When Jefferson left the table, Lillian jumped right on Valerie. "What happened? Why did you go cold on him so suddenly?"

Valerie looked disappointed as she shared. "He has a lady friend. He says he's available, but who knows if they will get back together. I see you like him huh, inviting him to your party?"

"Yes, I do like him. Go for it girl. The lady friend hasn't stopped him so far. There is definitely something going on between you two. I would not be surprised if you two were married by August," Lillian predicted. "Just let go and enjoy him."

As soon as Lillian left on Sunday, Valerie called Jefferson. She had called him late in the evening on

Thursday, Friday, and Saturday so she was trying to switch things up. He was busy with family for Game Day so they didn't talk long. He invited Valerie over but she declined, choosing instead to spend some time at home alone, thinking of Vincent and what that relationship being over really meant, and whether moving forward with Jefferson would be the right thing to do. Dinner on Monday would be a turning point.

Valerie had to admit that even though it had been over two years since they split up, she was still hurt and angry that Vincent had cheated. She had been a faithful and dutiful wife and mother, keeping herself active and vibrant and willing to please him. But underneath it all, she was unhappy. Unhappy that what excitement they did have in the early years had gone out of their marriage. She was bored, and angry that he didn't even notice or want to try new things that she suggested they do together. Ultimately, she was disappointed that she chose the quiet life with him and it still didn't end in happily ever after.

Valerie was curious about why Vincent was refusing to sign the divorce papers. Once the financial agreement was reached in February, he could have signed the divorce papers that same day, but he refused. Vincent requested more time for them to talk about the relationship and try to get back together. She didn't understand because she had nothing more to say and told that to him and the judge. Her opinion seemed not to matter because a sixty day continuance was granted, but with the court docket being full, their next court date had to be scheduled for ninety days. The divorce could be granted sooner if Vincent signed. They could avoid another court date.

Was he deliberately stalling? Some men liked being able to say they were still married to keep the girlfriend from getting ideas. Was he really interested in getting back together with Valerie? If so, would she be interested in getting back with him?

Before she met Jefferson, she thought about it but had decided that she was totally turned off with the idea of sleeping with Vincent after he had been with another woman. Could he do anything to help her get over that? Now she was curious about being with Jefferson. Maybe if she slept with him she would feel that she could deal with Vincent's affair and would consider getting back with him. She had no experience juggling two men so it was interesting to think about what that could mean.

Chapter Six

When Valerie arrived at her condominium, she checked her mail, changed clothes, and got comfortable on her sofa so she could really think some more about this proposed week with Jefferson.

The more she re-hashed the weekend of their meeting in her mind, the more she got excited about the possibilities with him. First the flowers on Thursday and then food for the staff on Friday. It was thoughtful and unusual. Was he a stalker? Did he have to see her every day and bring her gifts to overwhelm her into liking him? He was a handsome man who didn't seem to need to do anything extra to get the attention of women. Helen sure wanted him and yet it didn't sound like he had done anything like this for her. A few lunch dates sounded normal.

When he talked about his relationship with his ex-wife, the only type of grand gesture she heard was how hard he worked to pay all her medical school bills. That sounded more like a man who loved his wife and had a plan to put them in a good financial position by the time they were both out of school. What was she missing? Was he really the knight in shining armor that she needed to provide salve to the wounds she felt after her husband cheated? He was sexy and new. He could definitely put some good excitement in her life.

Valerie continued to stall for time to make a decision. She called Lillian, who repeated what she had said when she was in Houston: "Yes! Yes! Yes! Go for it." Then she added, "If it sours, at least you would have had the best time of your life. And if it's as good as it feels, hey, see where it goes."

She cleaned her apartment and washed clothes. She thought about calling her sister. Stephanie never liked Vincent so when Valerie finally filed for divorce, Stephanie all but threw her a party to celebrate her freedom. She would probably like a man like Jefferson for Valerie, but it was the middle of the workday and Stephanie was probably in one of a million meetings.

Finally, she called her daughter to see how she would feel about her mom getting into a relationship at this time, and so soon after meeting this new man. They usually talked every day so Nikki would not be surprised at the call. The topic, however, would be a first: her mom with a new man.

"I've met someone." Valerie let that bomb drop and waited for Nikki to respond. Nikki had never heard her talk about another man after the separation from Vincent. She knew there must be a reason for her to say that. Nikki could hear the hesitancy in her mom's voice so she asked to hear the full story of how they met, what he was like, and what had transpired in just a few days.

When Valerie was done, Nikki said quietly, "Go for it mom. I have been worried about you being alone and being busy but not being happy. You and dad had a good run, you were a great wife, and he was a jerk for what he did. You deserve a good man. And some real fun. Man fun. I can't wait to come home to meet him. Or for you guys to come visit. I love you. Be happy!"

Valerie said a prayer and packed work clothes, nightclothes, lounging clothes, and going out clothes to last for the week. Maybe two weeks. She would come home when he was at work if she needed to switch things up or get more.

She grabbed the Hydrangeas thinking that she and Jefferson could enjoy them at his house instead of the flowers wilting and dying at her place since she would not be there. Then she stopped at the store for a few things he did not have that she liked and headed for his house.

Promptly at five, he called to ask what she wanted for dinner. "Just come home. I've cooked," she responded. She was glad that she had because he sounded tired. He was surprised and arrived at six, walking in from the garage, dirty and thoroughly exhausted but very complimentary about the smell of the food. "I already know about your kissing skills. It smells like you've got skills in the kitchen as well Ms. Mason. A woman of many talents. I like that. I am hungry too. First, I need a shower. I'll be right back."

Valerie tried to stop him. "Before you go, will you do me a favor?"

He did not stop walking and asked, "Can it wait? I want to take a shower and clean up for dinner. I won't be long." There was no time for Valerie to respond he was out of the kitchen so fast. She thought to herself, first lesson learned: let him get his shower after work before asking him for anything.

He was back in the kitchen a few minutes later, clean, and now clearly agitated. "How was your day?" he asked as he sat at the end of the table looking around. He then focused on her, watching her closely.

"Good. Busy. Talked to Nikki. I always love to hear her voice. How about you? I know you are tired. Did you get everything on the schedule done today?" She gave him a cold beer and stood by him to get a hello kiss, listen to his response, and ask him the favor, but from the frown on his face, she knew he had something on his mind.

"Yes," he said slowly, twirling the bottle around on the table and looking at her with a mixture of confusion and disappointment. So much for a kiss, she thought.

"What's going on in that mind of yours Jefferson? What's wrong?" She couldn't imagine what could have happened since he had just walked in and gone straight to the shower.

He leaned toward her to respond. "We had a conversation this morning about you staying here for the week. I noticed that you didn't say anything so I guess it was just me talking. I was hoping that you were going to go home, pack, and come back. I've been in every room and every closet in this house and the only thing of yours in here is your purse. No luggage, no clothes in any closet, nothing. That one dress will not be enough for a week, so I guess you decided to come back but not stay. Why are you here? I don't need you to cook for me." He was perturbed.

Leaning to the side against the table, Valerie looked at him for a long time before responding.

"I'm going to give you a pass tonight since I know you are exhausted, but I really don't like your tone. Our first order of business in getting to know each other is to learn how to communicate so we don't push each other's buttons."

He did not break his stare.

She continued, "I'm very clear that I don't need to cook for you. I thought I was being kind since you worked all day and I did not. I figured you would be tired.

"As for me staying for the week…" she paused.

"Is my car still outside?" She asked with a tone of concern.

"Yes," was his quick, dry reply. "I parked my truck next to it."

"Well I asked you to do me a favor when you came in but you blew by me to get in the shower, and you have come back with an attitude. I wanted you to get my bag out of the trunk. I had groceries and the flowers you gave me in my arms when I came in and decided not to go back out. So yes, I am staying for the week."

She paused again, looking closely at him. "On second thought, maybe not since you're tired and mad. Not a problem." She turned off the stove and headed for the den to get her purse.

He quickly reached for her arm to pull her back into the kitchen and apologized. "I'm sorry.

I have been so anxious all day about whether you would come back then excited when I called and you said you were here. When I didn't see a bag, I was disappointed, and hurt that you didn't want to be with me." He asked for the key to her car.

"First," she said sternly, "you need to kiss me hello like you missed me. It's how we leave in the morning and come back together at night. Agreed?" She finally smiled at him.

"Agreed," he said quickly. "I like that." He kissed all over her face then landed on her lips, licking them with the tip of his tongue then slipping into her mouth searching for her tongue. She couldn't help but to kiss him back. You could feel the shift in the atmosphere from the tense conversation a moment ago to the heat of two people who liked being together.

After a couple of minutes, they broke apart and she reached into her pocket to give him the key fob so he could bring her bag inside. She shook her head thinking men are just tall, spoiled boys. Don't give them what they want and they pout. It made her smile though, knowing he was so anxious about her staying or thinking that she might leave.

Chapter Seven

She had a surprise for him so after dinner she asked him to go relax in bed while she cleaned the kitchen. "Make sure you go to the bathroom," she requested.

He looked at her with a question in his eyes. "You do remember that I am not the young stud I thought I was at one time and I'm exhausted tonight? Jimbo will not be rising to any occasion, not even for you, as much as I want to."

She paused for a moment, puzzled, then laughed and rolled her eyes. "So there is Jefferson, Jeannette, and Jason, and even the name for your penis starts with a J? Too much. Only Steven got a break, huh? I hope he doesn't feel left out."

He had a quick comeback. "Steven didn't get left out. His last name is Jackson. Besides, the Mason family had already taken the letter V so we just went higher up the alphabet. You know, in keeping with that synergy, my name for you will be V. Just V. V for Valerie. V for Valentine. V for the way your legs open for me." He gave her a sexy look that made her cheeks and a couple other body parts tingle.

"Just go. Take your shirt off and put on some shorts. And don't go to sleep." She was shaking her head. He was always finding a way to say something slick and sexy. She liked it. He made her laugh.

He was relaxed and scrolling through his phone in the bed when she walked into the bedroom. She turned the overhead light off, leaving the lamp on the dresser on, took the phone out of his hand and put it in the drawer of the nightstand. Then she threw the covers off him and told him to lay back and close his eyes. He did, then opened one eye to see what she was doing. When he saw a bottle in her hand and felt the warm oil on his skin, he sat up. "What are you doing?" He was surprised and unsure of what she was putting on his body.

"Just relax. It's massage oil. You have worked hard today and I want to help you sleep." She was in control and continued to rub him with long, slow strokes with the warm oil. He liked the way her hands felt and trusted her so he laid back down, keeping his eyes closed this time. No one had ever done this to him before but he was all in for the experience.

She massaged his feet, calves, and thighs, and even peeped at Jimbo. Liking what she saw, she gave him a stroke or two, eliciting a soft moan out of Jefferson. She finished by rubbing his chest and arms, then she asked him quietly in his ear to turn over.

Starting at his feet, she rubbed the back of his legs, rubbed his butt, then straddled him to rub his back and shoulders and neck. He was moaning loud and long for a few minutes. The more he relaxed, the softer he moaned, then silence and snores. She kissed him on the cheek and turned the light off as she left the room.

It was only eight o'clock so Valerie went to the den to read for a while. She got in bed with him around midnight but he did not move to acknowledge that she was there. He was in a deep, deep sleep.

Valerie woke up at seven the next morning, surprised that Jefferson was still asleep. He was usually up and having his coffee. She dressed for the day and headed to the den to wait for him to wake up. He obviously needed the rest so she was not going to disturb him.

At 7:30, she heard the lock on the front door buzz and the door open. She figured it had to be a family member with a code so she walked into the family room to greet them. In walked a tall, slender woman with Jefferson's nephew, Steven.

"Good morning," Valerie said to them both. "Good to see you again Steven." She assumed this was a regular visit.

Steven was pleasantly surprised to see her so early in the morning. "Hello again. You're the lady from the flower shop."

"Yes, I'm Valerie."

"Well this is my mom Jeannette, Uncle Jeff's sister." She looked closely at Jeannette who was a very beautiful woman, tall like Valerie, same warm chocolate color as Jefferson, same black eyes, with shoulder length black hair sprinkled lightly with gray. She realized Steven must look like his father. He was tall too, but with the café au lait color and light brown eyes. She thought he was quite a handsome young man and his son looked just like him.

"Hi Valerie. Where is my brother? He didn't answer my calls this morning and that never happens. Is he okay?" Her voice was gruff, challenging.

"Absolutely. He is asleep. He was exhausted after work so he ate and went to bed. Do you want to see him? Should I wake him up? Did you want to go to his room?" Valerie was gracious and respected their concern.

"No. If you say he's okay, I'll take you at your word. If you don't mind, I will have some coffee then head to work." Jeannette wanted to get to know who this Valerie woman was so she was prolonging the visit.

Steven was satisfied that his uncle was okay and his mother seemed relaxed after finding out her brother was okay. He left with a smile on his face, thinking of his uncle already with Ms. Valerie, in less than a week, and she had clearly spent the night. He considered that being a player of the highest order.

Valerie saw an opportunity to get to know Jeannette. "I haven't made coffee yet so maybe you can show me how you guys like it."

Valerie and Jeannette were chatting away when Jefferson walked into the kitchen with a faraway look in his eyes. He tapped Jeannette on the shoulder, said "Hey," then made a beeline for Valerie, pulling her out of the chair to give her a big hug, and pressing his lips on hers for a quick kiss. Still holding her, he sat in the chair with her standing between his legs and leaning back on him. Finally, he talked to his sister.

"So Jeannette, you've met my Valentine Love. What are you two chatting about?"

"You. Why didn't you answer my calls this morning? I thought something had happened to you. Steven just left for work. I had him come with me in case something was wrong." Jeannette was initially irritated but saw how he was acting with Valerie so she softened her tone. He seemed happier than she had seen him in a long time.

"Valerie took my phone last night and I haven't heard anything ringing this morning. I had the best sleep I've had in forever. How long have I been asleep?"

"Twelve hours," Valerie answered. Jefferson and Jeannette looked surprised. They looked at each other then back at Valerie.

"Okay Ms. Valerie," Jeannette said. "You must have some good stuff to knock my brother out for twelve hours. Do you give lessons?"

Valerie looked at Jefferson, shocked.

He laughed saying, "No, she has no filter either. It is part of the Ware charm." Then he shared with his sister that Valerie had given him his first massage. "That is some miracle working magic. Do you get massages Jeannette? Come to think of it, I've never heard you talk about them."

Jeannette frowned and responded, "I've had one but I didn't like a strange person rubbing on me. I was not comfortable and I never went back."

"Well I am so sorry for you because they are great. I am obsessed now with Valerie and her soft, wonderful hands."

Valerie and Jeannette looked at him with the expression of pure bliss on his face then looked at each other and laughed.

"So new house rules." Jefferson cleared his throat.

"Don't come busting in here unannounced. Valerie's going to be here so we might be busy. Like the old commercial said, phone first. If you don't get me, keep trying until you do. Better yet, take Valerie's number. She might answer her phone when I don't answer mine. I'll be sure to tell Steven. In fact, I'd better call him now."

Jeannette finished her coffee and took Valerie's number while Jefferson was on the phone, then she had a final comment for Valerie. "He likes you. A lot. Be gentle with him. He's a good guy and I don't want to see him hurt." She stared at Valerie as if to confirm that she meant her message which made Valerie chuckle. This family loves to stare, Valerie mused. She then told Jeannette, "I have no intentions of hurting him and I don't want to be hurt either so we should be good."

Jefferson walked Jeannette to the door and she told him how happy she was for him. "She seems nice, but I need to get to know her. If you like her, I'm sure I'll be good with her."

He responded quickly to Jeannette, "I like her a lot. So yes, get to know her."

Chapter Eight

After his sister left, Jefferson fixed breakfast. While eating, he and Valerie talked about what they wanted to do for the day. It was Tuesday so Valerie did not have to work and Jefferson's schedule was light so he asked Ron to take all of the jobs.

"I don't get to do this often. Could we just go back to bed? Not to sleep, and no, not even for sex. I want to stretch out so we can relax and talk." Jefferson had things to tell her and to ask her.

Valerie nodded yes. She liked the idea that they would have the day to themselves.

Jefferson had made the bed when he got up so he pulled the pillows out from under the cover and sat on the bed with his back on the pillows against the headboard, legs stretched out in front of him. She sat on his right but in the middle of the bed, turned so that she could face him. She had on shorts and a tank top so she sat cross-legged, then put her elbows on her knees.

His first question made them both laugh. "Where in this city do you live? I have no idea how to find you except at the flower shop. If you left here angry with me or something happened to you and the shop was not open, I would have no idea where or how to find you. In fact, put your address in my phone right now."

She did as he asked then offered, "You know you could come and stay at my place sometime. I don't have a nice big house like this anymore, just a three bedroom condo, but I would be happy for us to hang out there too."

"Yes, let's do that. I want to see how you live. What your place says about you. And what it would take to get all of you moved in here."

She shook her head. "Jefferson, could we get through one week together first before you have me packed up and squeezing into your already full house? By Friday we might not be speaking. If you come at me with an attitude like you did last night, I can guarantee you that we won't be."

She was smiling when she said it, but she meant it. She could handle a good verbal tangle, but did not like people, especially men, to speak to her in a mean, nasty way.

"I got your message loud and clear Ms. Mason. I just wanted to be with you." He returned her serious look then winked at her.

"Since we're on the subject, V, what other hot buttons do you have? Deal breakers? Piss you off topics?" He wanted to avoid as many landmines as possible.

She thought about it for a minute then said, "Don't lie to me, please. I need to be able to trust you and if I catch you in a lie, or find out that you lied, I have a hard time forgiving that."

"Along with that, don't talk to me like I'm stupid. It's disrespectful." She was having some flashbacks of conversations with Vincent before she put him out of the house. "My husband kept denying that he was cheating even though I had hotel receipts and his clothes often smelled of someone else's cologne. I had seen him with the woman at lunch when he thought I was at work. I made sure he saw me but didn't confront him in the restaurant. When he got home that night, his clothes were on the floor in the family room floor waiting for him to pack and leave."

Jefferson was shaking his head in agreement. "I get it. I feel the same way."

"Don't cheat on me," she continued. "If you find someone else attractive and you want to pursue her, then let me know so that I can get out of your way. I always want to believe that our relationship is special, sacred, so if someone else can get your attention, it means that either you are a selfish pig, or that you don't want me anymore. Or both. So let me go to someone who will treasure me."

He was agreeing again, only this time he said, shaking his head, "You don't have to worry about that. I can already see that you are a handful, more than enough for me so I will not be cheating. And if I catch you cheating on me I will kill you and him so that will be the end of our story." He was smiling when he said it to let her know he was joking, then reached over and pretended to choke her, kissing her while he had her close.

"So what are your deal breakers, hot buttons, Mr. Jefferson Ware?"

"I agree with what you just said about lying and cheating. Trust is a big deal to me too. Even all these years after Alicia, I am still sensitive about not being wanted and I don't like that feeling. I have to trust that you mean what you say when you say that you care about me. I would have a hard time getting over that if it happened again. Women aren't the only ones who get hurt."

He paused, thinking of whether there was anything else he wanted to say. "One more thing. I don't like to fight. We have to be able to talk things out. Communication is everything to me. Like last night, the way you handled the way I came at you. It was classy and kept things from escalating cause I was getting plenty mad at the idea of not being able to sleep with you again."

"Oh, you mean when spoiled five year old Jeffy came home from school yesterday and couldn't play with his favorite toy?" She had to tease him. He really had pouted.

He reached over to pull her up to him and nuzzled her neck saying, "Yes, because you are my favorite everything now, and I want to play with you all day every day." Then he held her hands and asked about the massage.

"Where did you learn to do that? It felt so good. It felt like you were talking to me with your hands, telling me to relax but also saying that you cared about me, Jefferson Ware, cared that I was tired and needed to be touched to feel whole again. I slept for twelve hours so that should prove how much I needed that. How often can I get one of those? Every week?" His look was playful, but he was serious.

"Well, it clearly has to be a night when you are off the next day. I would hate to wake you up before the 12th hour of your renewal slumber."

"Please don't. That was the best sleep; and twelve hours? I never sleep that long. So do you like massages too? I want to see how you react when I give you one." He already loved rubbing her back. To get to do that to the rest of her in bed would feel like New Year's Eve fireworks in his body.

"As a matter of fact, I do." The faraway look on her face was like his and said it all. "I try to get to a spa for a massage every month or two. I guess I can save that money now if you are going to give them to me."

"Oh yes. Happy to put that on my "honey do" list." He was rubbing her leg while he talked to show how willing he was. He liked touching her. She smiled to let him know she liked being touched. She liked the way he rubbed her neck and back when she was fully clothed so to strip down for a massage that he would give her…she could hardly wait.

They took a bathroom break and sat back on the bed, this time side by side. He held her hand.

"Next question: Were the folks at the flower shop impressed with my grand gestures to you?"

"Oh yes! You definitely have a fan club at Fay's Flowers."

"Good," he replied. "So are you the president of my fan club?"

"We didn't get quite that far. I think Billy would like that title, he's so enamored with you." She was laughing, thinking of how the whole staff decided she should hook him and never let him go.

He paused for a moment then said, "I'm sure Billy is nice, but I want you to be the president, my champion."

"We will have to see about that," she said, trying not to sound too easy.

"Okay, now tell me what did Lillian say about me? Did she approve?" He was rubbing her palm then the back of her hand.

"Oh, yes." Valerie laughed and admitted, shaking her head, "She has us married by the time of their anniversary party. Said she could feel the heat waves between us and she likes you for me."

Jefferson was excited to hear that and told Valerie, "I knew I liked her! She must have been reading my mind. Let's get them an extra special anniversary gift."

She decided to say something that had been bothering her since their lunch. "I owe you an apology."

"For what? We haven't known each other that long to already have to apologize for anything. What is it?" His voice was comforting.

"When Lillian asked you about coming to their anniversary party, I didn't handle that well. I was surprised that she said it, and nervous that you would think we were trying to say that I knew we would be together in August. That's six months away. I would not want you to think I was being presumptuous, especially for a week-end trip."

He laughed quietly. "You can be presumptuous. I already expect that we will be together in August and can make the trip. Lillian's nice. I would like to meet her husband."

Valerie was nodding okay, happy to hear that he wanted them to be together for a while. He continued with his questions, still holding her hand. "Now I've got the flower shop family rooting for me and Lillian. Who is next? Oh, yes. Did you tell your sister about me? About us?"

"I haven't told my sister yet. She will be happy that I have moved on from Vincent. She never liked him and always kept her distance. She liked his brother Victor better for me because he was nice looking and smart too, but more fun, but by the time she met him, I was already marrying Vincent."

"And Nikki?" He asked, very curious about her reaction to her mother with another man.

"Yes, I told Nikki. She said she was happy for me to be with someone who was so nice. She wanted to know if you made me laugh. I said yes. She said then go all in and enjoy."

"When will I get to meet her?" He knew she was important to Valerie making a decision to be with him so the sooner the better.

"She will probably be home again in a month or so, definitely for Memorial Day. She always comes home for holidays. In the meantime, she said we are welcome to visit her and Checkers, anytime."

Jefferson was curious about the name. "Checkers?"

"Yes, her baby. My grand dog. He's a black and white Lhasa Apso."

"Do you like dogs? Or cats? Would you want us to have one?" He was actually open to having one to complete their family.

"Dogs. Never cats. Maybe we could, just not right away." She realized she was also speaking of their future together. While it surprised her, it was okay.

Jefferson's phone rang and it was Ron so he answered. Ron had several questions about the repairs on a couple of the homes he was working on that day so Jefferson told Valerie, "Don't go anywhere," and went into the family room to talk. When he came back into the bedroom, Valerie way lying down scrolling through her phone. He positioned himself on the bed so that they were lying side by side. They turned to face each other, eager to continue the conversation.

Chapter Nine

"So what is Nikki like?" He enjoyed the way Valerie's eyes lit up when he mentioned her daughter's name. He hoped that he was making her eyes light up for him too. He rubbed her eyebrows with his thumb and watched her lips move as she talked. He was ready to kiss again but knew this conversation was important to get them on solid footing in knowing each other. He waited and smiled, very obvious that he was enjoying watching her, especially her lips.

"Nikki is sweet, smart, and headstrong. Comfortable in her own skin. She can be a talker too. She was an easy pregnancy and birth and we adored her. We tried to temper our delight in her by making her learn that she could not get everything she asked for, and she had to learn to share her toys and work for what she wanted."

"We never tried to have more children so of course she is spoiled, and a daddy's girl until she found out he cheated on me. On us. She was very angry with him for destroying our family and took it hard when I put him out. They are slowly repairing their relationship."

"So what really happened with you and your husband? Cheating usually comes when something else has gone haywire. What was it for you, V?"

He wanted to know more about her husband and how he could cheat on such a loving and classy woman. Or if there was something about Valerie he needed to know that spoke of her lack of ability to be in a long term relationship.

"The truth is I probably should not have married him. He was the stereotype that all parents want for their children: nice looking, kind to my folks, educated, and ready to get married and focus on his family and career.

"We met in a restaurant. I was on a date and he was out with some work friends. I should have known then what kind of man he was. He hit on me when my date went to the men's room. At the time, I thought he was just bold and aggressive and it made me feel like he knew what he wanted and was not afraid to go for it."

She sat up on the side of the bed then moved to the chair in the room to continue with her story. She was starting to feel agitated but wanted to be honest with Jefferson. In addition, it felt weird to talk about Vincent while she was in bed with another man so she decided to move off the bed. Jefferson watched her, noticing the change in her mood and wondered why she sat in the chair. He sat up on the side of the bed and asked if she was okay. She nodded yes, but he kept watching her to see what she might do next. She finished the story.

"He did all the right things to wine and dine me. We went to the nicest restaurants, art shows, his work events, trips to Europe. We were a couple at all the family gatherings on both sides. Everyone assumed we would get married. It was just a matter of time."

"We dated for two years then he asked me to marry him while we were vacationing in Paris. I didn't say yes right away. That should have been a sign. My sister hated him. She thought he was cocky with nothing to offer to match his attitude. Another sign. He was nice and I enjoyed his company, but when I looked at Lillian and Max, I could see a different level of happiness than what I was feeling for Vincent. There was no "magic," just a comfort level that my mom and my sister said was normal. Even my married friends said that he was a good package being educated, upwardly mobile, and a family man. I couldn't think of a reason to say no. Eventually I said yes and we had a small wedding in Hawaii with about twenty family and friends.

"After we got married, our lives quickly settled into a routine of work for both of us, especially long hours for him trying to get promoted and make more money. A lot of the outside dates and activities stopped, except appearances for his work events and birthdays and anniversaries. We were planning that I would not work at all or just work part time when we had children.

"Then Nikki came along. He was a great dad -- when he was home. I loved Nikki, but I missed my husband and he never could understand what I had to complain about since I had every material thing I needed and all that we wanted to give Nikki. Ultimately, I think we both grew up and grew apart over the years. I know I got lonely. One day I realized I was actually bored with him. I wanted more in my husband and in my life."

"Did you like being married?" Jefferson was already thinking of her as his wife.

"Yes, I did," she smiled. "I don't miss him, but I miss having the relationship, the companionship, the love. I even miss the fun that comes with knowing someone close like that, sharing your day to day life and creating memories together." Valerie wondered if this would be a good time to tell him that the divorce was not final, deciding it might ruin the good mood she was feeling so she decided to wait for another day.

"Okay V, my last question, but it's a two-parter. How long has it been since you had sex or made love—whatever you call it-- and when was the last time you were tested?"

Valerie leaned to the side as if being knocked over by a strong wind. She had not expected such a direct set of questions so soon.

He saw her surprise and commented: "I'll share with you too so don't think I'm just being nosey."

"I don't know if I know the difference between having sex and making love. Isn't it all the same?" Val queried.

Jefferson was happy to provide his definition for her. "Sex to me is a practical experience. I'm horny, you're horny, we get together and take care of each others needs. A lot of times people then go on with the rest of their lives, separately, until it happens again. I think that's what the term "fuck buddies" was invented to describe. Sometimes couples have sex because its expedient and they don't have time for foreplay or a relationship.

"Making love is taking our time to get to know each other and establish a relationship so that when we are together there's emotion, intimacy. I want to make love to you."

"Okay. Well, the last time was about three years ago, just about the time I confirmed my husband had cheated. I got tested right away to be sure he had not done anything stupid like bringing some disease home." She was slightly embarrassed but decided the truth was the truth.

Jefferson was pleasantly surprised. Three years? He was happy that she had not been with anyone since her husband, but it made him curious so he asked another question: "Do you like making love? Or were you turned off from that after he cheated?"

She couldn't look at him as she confessed. "I enjoy making love. To be honest Jefferson, I am not that experienced. There had only been a couple of guys before Vincent. After a few years of marriage and a baby, sex became a part of our routine but there were no fireworks or X-rated movies being made."

Finally satisfied that he knew enough, he made his own confession. "The last time I had sex was about four or five months ago, and I used condoms. I got tested right after anyway. I just want to know where we stand before we explore this fire that's smoldering between us."

He got quiet and looked at her until she looked up at him.

"Are you okay? What are you thinking?" he asked.

"Nothing." The truth was she was even more curious now about how they would be together. He was very sexy to her already so if the heat they were both feeling was real feelings, there was no telling what would happen. She stifled a laugh as she envisioned her head exploding like in a cartoon from the power of making love with him.

"So do you have condoms for all the love making you're planning for us to do?" she asked quietly.

He leaned over to pull open the nightstand drawer and threw a bag at her. There was a receipt stapled to the outside, dated Monday when she came over for dinner. Inside was a big box of condoms. She looked at the box then at him, commenting, "Wow. Got plans to be busy Mr. Ware?"

"Yes, in fact I do. All with you. All in due time." His look was matter-of-fact. Her only response was to put the bag back in the drawer and close it gently while smiling to herself. She liked the way he thought and was even more interested in moving in that direction.

Chapter Ten

She had questions of her own so she got water for them from the kitchen then sat on the side of the bed to ask. "So what are you looking for in a lady friend?" He was happy to share. "After my divorce, it took a couple of years to deal with the rejection, but then I opened myself up again to relationships and love.

"I always evaluated the women I was attracted to against my checklist: she had to be intelligent because I like to talk about a variety of topics. She had to be a little thick and like to eat. I'm a big guy and like to cook and eat, and skinny women were often too focused on their weight to enjoy a good meal. She had to be independent, both in the way she lived her life and financially. I do not want someone who is "needy" so that she has to be with me 24/7, or broke so she needs me to take care of her. I will take care of my wife. I just want her to have her own life already so we blend. I don't want to take care of someone else and get burned again.

"She has to have a sense of humor and like to have fun, enjoying family and friends and creating good times and good memories. Most of all, she has to really be into me. Not for what I have or can do for her, but for who I am, and would enjoy the two of us being together whether hanging out at home or being out and about.

"In my thirties, I dated a lot. I completed my engineering degree and worked at a firm with a few women who either wanted to date me or they wanted to introduce me to their girlfriends or family. I didn't believe in playing where I got paid so I agreed to meet a few of the friends and family. No one special in the group.

"In my forties, I decided I did not want the corporate life anymore and chose to work for myself, driving trucks cross country and helping a friend in his moving business. Eventually I set up my own company that included real estate, doing electrical work, maintenance, and building repair projects.

"I met a couple of nice ladies through the years and dated each one for a year or so but there was always something missing. Both relationships ended amicably. I never found the one who made me want to try marriage again. I always kept my focus on work and helping to raise Steven and now Jason." He paused to gauge her reaction to his comments. She was thinking that he sounded honest and shared more than she expected.

"How do you think your family will feel about you being with one woman after all of these years?" She was thinking of how Jeannette came in to the house so stern and challenging. Maybe she really was worried about her brother and not judging Valerie.

"They will be happy for me I hope. If not, too bad. They are not here late at night when I can't sleep and am wishing for a special lady to share my bed and my life. We will soon find out though now that you are here."

"Okay Mr. "I've got condoms because we're going to be busy." Here's one for you. Natural or waxed? Do you have a preference?"

He looked at her head then frowned, not understanding the question. When it registered what she meant, he tried to lift her shorts so he could look, asking, "What have you got under there?"

She swatted his hand away. "Just answer the question."

He did. "I don't have a preference. I'm old school so I'm used to natural. If what's down there is anything like what is on your head, I vote that you please keep it. I love your hair. But if you prefer waxed, have at it." He paused, then asked, curious, "So what do you have under there?" He pulled on her shorts again and she slapped his hand again, telling him, "That will be a surprise for you. No sneak peeks."

The conversation had gotten so personal it was making them both warm and curious. They decided to take a break from the interrogation and go to the den to watch a movie, falling asleep.

It was leftovers for dinner after which they tried watching another movie in the bedroom. This time they finished it, and read in bed until after midnight. They were about to go to sleep for the night when he realized it was Thursday -- one week to the day he walked into the flower shop and his life changed. He decided to tell her his feelings.

"Hey, happy one week anniversary! Thank you for being here V. This has been a very special week for me."

"Yes," she agreed thoughtfully, "It has been nice. Very nice."

They turned the lights off and she moved into his arms. He was on his back and her body was half on his, her leg resting in between his.

"I'm falling in love with you Valerie Mason. Dream of us." He said it quietly as he wrapped his arm around her and drifted off to sleep.

She heard his light snore and was glad she did not have to respond.

What could she say to that? She really, really was enjoying him and wanted more time with him. At her age, though, and with one divorce soon to be under her belt, she did not want to jump in too soon and end up not together because they did not take the time to get to know each other, and once they did, realized they did not like each other.

She was restless throughout the night and he could feel her moving around, never seeming to find a comfortable position. They had already established a pattern, sleeping as if there were magnets in their bodies that kept them touching each other somewhere throughout the night. If she turned over onto her stomach, his hand reached over to rest on her butt. If he turned over, she threw her leg on him or backed into him or their feet touched.

He felt her body constantly shifting. He figured it was because of what he said and smiled. He had a strong suspicion that she was wrestling with her own feelings, which meant just maybe she was falling in love with him too.

From Jefferson's experience, women were often hesitant to say the "L" word first, and to hear it in a week's time put a lot of pressure on them. Conservative, thoughtful women like Valerie probably needed at least six months to feel she knew enough about a person to be comfortable saying she loved him.

He wasn't worried though. They were both at an age where they recognized the limitations of time and longevity so they needed to enjoy each other as much as possible for as long as possible. At least that was his hope.

She was excited to hear that he was falling for her. She knew, however, that she needed to tell him the status of the divorce before things went too much further. She didn't want him to feel that she was hiding anything from him or not being truthful. At the same time, she knew that she needed to speak with her lawyer to find a way to speed things up now that she had a reason to be single and available.

Jefferson was tempted to make love to her to get her relaxed but decided to let her wrestle with her feelings and come to a conclusion without him putting pressure on her. He knew it was time to step up trying to get her to commit to him.

Chapter Eleven

Thursday morning came and they prepared to go to work. He was up first and drinking his coffee when she came in the kitchen. Both were dressed for the day. She went directly to the refrigerator for water.

He opened his arms for her to come to him and she went with a smile. That seemed to establish their morning ritual. Touching. Loving. Kissing. A great way to start the day.

He showed her his work schedule then asked what she does with her time after work and on days that she does not work.

"Usually during the week after work I head to the grocery store or run other errands which makes for a full day. Then on my days off, I can be at home relaxing, making calls, or having lunch with friends. Sometimes I go shopping or to a museum."

Jefferson was excited to hear what she liked to do and made an offer. "I would love to go to museums with you. And art shows and plays as well as a jazz club or two. Plus we can try new restaurants. I like all those things, but haven't been going a lot lately because I got tired of going by myself. The only thing is we would have to go mostly on the weekends since a lot of my weekdays are busy. Are you okay with that?"

Valerie was happy to accept. "I like that. I get tired of going by myself too sometimes so this will be fun. Thanks." She was impressed that they liked the same things and that they could be together regularly.

"If you haven't been going out, then what have you been doing with your free time Mr. Entrepreneur Ware?"

"Not much. During the week in the evening, I'm home, reading or watching television. Every month I meet up with some guys from the Air Force or one of my old jobs. On the weekends, I mostly hang out with the family. I get a head and beard shave every Friday. We get together at Jeannette's on Saturday mornings for family meetings. Game Day is here on Sundays. Jeannette, Steven, Jason, and sometimes Ann, Jason's godmother, will come for Game Day. Steven's wife died so Ann keeps Jason during the week while Steven works. She and Jason's mother were best friends so she's been around the family a long time. We watch whatever sport is in season on television or play table games. Will you be okay with Sunday's being family day?"

She knew this was an important time for their family and she was happy to be a part of it. Even Nikki would fit in since Vincent had made her a big sports fan.

"You know V, we should celebrate our one week together. I would like to finally take you out on a date. How about tomorrow? Our first official date."

"Okay." She liked the idea. "Where will we go? What will we do?" She wondered what he had in mind.

"I'll surprise you. Unless there is someplace you have wanted to go?"

"No. You decide. I like your surprises."

When Jefferson got home that night, he brought dinner from *Hillstone's Restaurant* and *Crave Cupcakes* for their anniversary dessert. He surprised her with a silver necklace with the letter V in the center and a card that said he was craving her.

Valerie was already at his house and had bought him a card and an oversized coffee mug that she had found imprinted with the words, "Your voice is my favorite sound." On the back, she had a large, fancy letter V imprinted in gold.

They made a toast at dinner. He spoke first.

"This has been the best week I have had in years and it's all because of you. I never thought I would feel this way at this time in my life and I am excited to see how next week and the weeks after unfold with us together. Happy Anniversary my Valentine Love."

She responded in kind. "Thank you for renewing my joy in the possibilities of a friendship, a relationship, maybe even love. You are one of a kind, and I'm very glad for this time with you. Happy one week anniversary!"

Both of them had worked that day so they had a quiet evening talking about their date.

Jefferson asked, "How about I pick you up at your place and spend the night there?" Surprise number one.

"Yes, let's do that," she said. They went to the bedroom so he could pack a bag to have at her place.

He announced, "The attire for the evening is dressy but not formal. Wear a dress, I'll be in a sports jacket and dress slacks." She was intrigued.

That is all he would share. The rest would unfold after he picked her up.

They went to bed happy about their celebration and looking forward to the next day.

She was restless again that night so he tried talking to her while rubbing her back.

"What's wrong V? This is the second night you have not been able to sleep. Are you feeling okay?"

She hesitated, thinking that maybe it would sound better if she said she felt sick, but then he would probably worry. "Yes, I'm okay."

"Then what's wrong? Is there something on your mind? Are you upset because of what I said last night?"

Valerie was nervous but replied honestly, "I don't know. Sort of. You excite me and overwhelm me and I am thoroughly enjoying you, but I'm afraid at the same time. I've never felt this energy that is between us with anyone before, and it's also been a long time since I've had sex so I don't know if it's love or lust."

Jefferson smiled and said to her while kissing her ear and neck, "Oh. Okay. Well, let's see if I can help you figure it out. Love is already in the air for me so let's see about the lust."

He rolled over on top of her and gave her long, deep tongue kisses that she felt to her toes. He played with her, pulling his tongue out as if he was done kissing, leaving her wanting more. She missed it immediately and went in search for it with her own tongue. He pinned her to the bed so she couldn't move. All she could do was open her mouth and legs to him and moan.

"I love kissing you," he whispered. "Your lips are soft and they mold exactly to mine. I like to lick your lips and tongue because you taste good and you know how to lick and suck my tongue right back. I could kiss you all night. I know we will be good together because our kisses are so good."

He proceeded to kiss her all over her ears and neck and shoulders and his lips found their way to her breasts. One by one he sucked her nipples while his hand moved between her legs.

He began to rub her slowly, feeling her get wet so he slid two fingers inside and continued to rub her very gently outside with his thumb.

His lips never stopped going from one breast, one nipple to the other, back and forth until he could feel her muscles tighten around his fingers and she called for him.

"Jeff," she moaned. "Oh Jeff. So good. So good."

He kissed her in the mouth again and pulled his fingers out. She reached down into his pants and asked if he was going to let Jimbo come out and play with her. She could feel how hard he was and she was ready to see if he would fit inside her. He was bigger at rest than some men were when they were hard.

"Please Jeff," she said softly in his ear, knowing it would give him that stroking feeling again.

His whole body responded instantly.

He pushed her legs apart and knees up with her thighs in a 'v' shape. He slid all the way inside her in one slow movement.

He looked in her eyes with that steady gaze and watched her face. She looked in his eyes too until she could feel that he had entered her completely. The feeling of fullness was overwhelming. She had to close her eyes as her body adjusted to his size and then his motion as he slid in and out. He was filling her like no one else had ever done.

She thought there was only one "G spot," but he was touching her in several other places that made her breathe heavy.

She wrapped her arms and legs around him and squeezed him, kissing his neck as she called for him. "Jeff," she whispered.

He whispered back to her, "Yes V. You feel so good. I feel like I'm in a vice, hot and tight and so wet. This is incredible."

They moved slowly in sync for a long while. It had been some time for both of them and neither were in a hurry to let it end.

Valerie could feel her body begin to vibrate. She knew what was about to happen. Again! He started moving inside her with a force that made her feel lightheaded. In no time, he was riding his own wave, moaning like he did when she gave him the massage. She rode another wave of her own, holding him tight, saying quietly, "Oooh, God help me."

When she was quiet again, he stopped moving and looked in her eyes, smiling. She smiled back at him.

He whispered in her ear, "Now Jimbo is in love with you too." He kissed her with the same intensity that he had just been pushing inside her, while wrapping his arms around her. They kissed for the longest time, both feeling a high that no alcohol or drug could give.

"So what do you think V? Did that feel like love or lust?"

She giggled. "It felt like really good lust. I don't know Mr. Ware. You are amazing. Love might have to wait until I get a lot more of you and Jimbo. That might take a while."

He laughed and assured her, "There's lots more where that came from so you can do both at the same time. I can almost guarantee that the lust will feel even better when you love me."

Just before he headed to the bathroom, he said it again. "I am falling in love with you Valerie Mason. And just so you know, my goal in the next few weeks is to get you to love me too."

"Jefferson. It's been a week." She put her head down in her hand but was smiling.

"Why are you so stuck on time? We are too old for "testing the waters." You are not the type to play games. I know exactly what I like and don't like and what I want and don't want. The likes and wants? They would all be you. Every part of you. We will reveal the rest to each other as we go along."

When he came out of the bathroom, he had more to say.

"Plus, I have a feeling that something is moving in that exact direction in your head. Or you wouldn't be here. Or so restless. I'm just saying. You're thinking it. I'm willing to put it out there."

He rubbed her leg as she was getting up to take her turn in the bathroom and asked her to hurry back. "You have worn me out and I'm ready to go to sleep. I can't do that now unless you are laying on me."

On the inside, Valerie was ready to shout she was so happy. She knew that she loved him too already with his constant displays of affection and tenderness. And Jimbo? O.M.G. She just could not let her hunger for him overshadow her rational mind.

When she got back in bed she laid on his chest and put her leg in between his as usual, but this time she put her hand down his pants, giving Jimbo a good night rub then wrapping her hand around him.

Jefferson whispered, "I like this sexy side of you. And I don't mind being whipped so have your way with me."

"Jefferson!" She acted as if she was embarrassed or appalled but she liked that she could express herself sexually with him. She did not have a lot of experience with men, and none of them made her feel as free and sexy as Jeff.

"I'll keep that in mind." Valerie snuggled closer and they both slept hard through the night.

Chapter Twelve

Jefferson got up early Friday and straightened up the tools, wood, and buckets that were on the side of the garage next to his Mercedes. He wanted Valerie to be able to drive her car into the garage and put the door down, a safety measure so she would not have to be exposed to outside people or bad weather.

When she walked into the kitchen that morning, she was glowing. Happy. Feeling sexy and loved. She walked directly over to him and put her arms around him, leaning in for a kiss.

"Hmmm. That good, huh?" he asked, happy too. "Is this your way of telling me you liked what we did and want more?" He was teasing her, but he was also curious about her sexuality.

"Mmm hmm," she groaned. "A lot more." She was feeling sexy and sassy. Jefferson had made her feel like a vibrant, lusty woman. Vincent had never made her feel like this. He wasn't much for kissing and sex with him was very traditional. He got the job done, but didn't leave her wanting more. At least not for him. She was already hot for Jeff again.

He put his hands under her skirt and cupped her butt cheeks. He pushed her panties to the side so he could be free to explore, letting his fingers find their way between her legs.

He caressed her and said, "Me too. We have lots to learn about each other. Favorite positions. How many times I can make you whisper my name in my ear. Whether I can make you scream. Or if you can make me scream." They both laughed at that.

She moved away from him to compose herself before leaving. She noticed the garage door opener on the table and asked what was wrong with it, why was it in the house.

"Put this in your car so you can pull into the garage from now on instead of parking in the drive-way. That way you are not exposed if you come home late or the weather is bad." He was already protecting her.

He dropped her off at her apartment with plans to come back for her at five for their date. They had one last kiss then prepared to go about their day. He had meetings and needed to get a haircut and she had a hair appointment at her favorite salon about ten minutes away. She always walked to her appointments unless the weather was bad. Both were excited to be going out that night as a couple.

When Valerie opened the door for their date, she was excited about how good he looked dressed up. She had only seen him in casual clothes and his work clothes throughout the week and he looked great in those. Tonight he took his sexy up a notch. He had a fresh head shave and beard trim and smelled good with a light fragrance that smelled like sunshine and being outdoors fresh. His suit looked like it was high quality, something from the Tom Ford label based on the cut. She loved men's clothes and shoes. Vincent was a very nice dresser so she was familiar with the brands.

He could not stop staring at her. She was definitely dressed to impress, showing just enough cleavage to be noticed but not trashy, and showing off her big shapely legs in a simple fitted knee length red dress with a flared tail and red high heels. She looked classy and sexy. The night was off to a good start.

She gave him the quick tour of her apartment and he noticed that all of her furniture looked new. She explained why. "When I sold the house, I sold all the furniture that was in it. I wanted no reminder of our life together, and Nikki didn't want any of it either."

She didn't have a lot, preferring a minimalist look, simple, very few accessories. A sofa and a couple of armchairs and side tables completed the living room. There was a bed and nightstands with a dresser for the tv in her bedroom and guest room/ Nikki's room, and a desk, small bookcase, and small loveseat in her office. Jefferson was already trying to figure out what each of them would have to get rid of to mix some of her furniture with his.

He loved her view of the city from the 17th floor. He stood at the floor to ceiling windows and said he was glad to be spending the night so he could see the moon and the city lights when they got back.

Valerie gave Jefferson a key to her condo. On the way out, they stopped at the front desk so Valerie could introduce Jefferson to the doorman and maintenance man on the evening shift. She put him on the list of people who had free access to her apartment, and asked them to let the day and midnight shifts know. She did the same with the garage attendant. It was her way of letting him know that he had full access to her place, just as she had at his house.

They had reservations at *Hugo's*, a five star, white tablecloth restaurant serving Mexican food. There was a trio playing Spanish music and the atmosphere was quiet elegance. They played *Happy Anniversary* to Valerie and Jefferson, and got a kick out of the fact that it had only been a week but they looked so in love. It was cozy and a great place to celebrate.

They spent a lot of time going over the menu to decide what to order. Jefferson convinced Valerie to try something new so she went for the octopus. He ordered the shrimp so that in case she did not like the octopus she could eat something more familiar.

Once their order was placed, Valerie asked about his day and his business. She realized she knew nothing more than the fact that he was an engineer and he went to houses a couple of days a week to do repairs and rebuild and replace things, especially when people moved out. It seemed like an odd package.

"When did you start your business? How does it work—you have a contract with the company that sends you assignments and that's what you read every morning? You don't seemed pressed to work every day so how do you make money?"

He looked at her for a long time then decided he should tell her the whole story. "I am a real estate investor. The homes I go to are the homes I own, about thirty or so altogether, mostly in Westchase, a few in Third Ward. I also own the property management company that sends me the assignments. They take the rental applications, requests for service, and the rent money for me and a few other real estate companies. I have a landscaping service that renters are required to use to make sure the yards are kept up. It was actually Jeannette's husbands business that I bought from her after he died. Me and Ron do the house repairs so I know the homes are up to code and well maintained. The renters don't know that I am also the owner."

He paused, watching her face to see if she would mentally start counting his money for what he could do for her as he had seen a few women do. Her expression didn't change. She was more surprised and curious than anything.

"I don't work nine to five every day because I don't have to. I help out when we get a lot of calls or a move out or a big job like on Tuesday when we had to replace the water heater. I get a status report on Fridays and meet with the management company once a month to go over the rentals and the money. I check on the landscaping company by riding around a couple of times a week and the management company pays them. If we have to put someone out, which is rare, I call my friend I used to work for who has a moving company and we get the job done. I also am a partner in a 200 unit apartment complex in Galveston with a couple of friends from engineering school and we meet once a month as well."

She nodded at him then commented, "Very nice. And smart. I like the way you set things up to keep the money circulating back to you."

He knew that her numbers mind would appreciate that.

"That's why I'm glad you are good at math and do what you do for Fay. When we get married you can help me with the business."

She paused when she heard him say married, making a mental note to think about the possibilities of that at another time. Then she slapped his hands playfully. "Don't be looking for work for me. You're smart and successful without me. I'm just glad to understand your schedule and know how to plan time for us to do things together. That was a challenge when I was married."

Their food came and they said grace and spent a few minutes eating in silence. He tasted her octopus and she ate one of his shrimp. Both were satisfied with the choices.

When she asked about the plans for the rest of the night, he still would not tell, only that they had to be at their next stop by eight.

"You like teasing me, making me wait. You need to know that I am very impatient and this is driving me crazy. I'll give you a pass tonight. It's fun."

She started guessing what their next stop would be. "The ballet? The theatre? A jazz club?" He never said yes or no, just laughed at her guesses and enjoyed watching her get excited.

Chapter Thirteen

The big surprise of the night was their visit to *Houston's Ballroom Dance*. Jefferson had signed them up for a Salsa class! Salsa is a sexy, fun dance that neither knew how to do. They both loved to dance, however, so this was perfect. They had a grand time learning all the steps and hip swinging and twirling moves, and pulling in close into each other's arms.

There were several other people there, mostly married couples but some singles, all learning Salsa, the Bachata, and other dances. After the class was over, they realized they wanted to come back again so they immediately signed up for more sessions. They had both worked up an appetite to make love again. It felt like the dancing was good foreplay so why not continue with more lessons?

They ended the night in her living room, on the sofa, in the dark, looking out at the city lights and drinking wine--a whole bottle of wine. They were feeling good, relaxed, and happy to be together.

She told him again that she had a great time and enjoyed his surprises. He reminded her that he liked to be thanked with a kiss so she straddled him and leaned in to kiss him while unbuttoning his shirt. She wanted to kiss his chest, rub and lick his nipples, and feel all over his body.

He was surprised that she didn't lead him to the bedroom, but he was ready for whatever she had in mind. She was in charge again and he liked it.

"I want to make love to you in the moonlight with all of the city watching." She was giggling and feeling naughty.

She did a little dance as she took off her dress and bra, surprising him when he saw she did not have on panties. She disrobed him: first, his shirt, then his pants and underwear, then socks and shoes. She was on her knees by the time she was finished and Jimbo was bobbing in her face so she said hello to him and rubbed him very slowly. Her hands were so soft that Jefferson could only moan and tell her how good her hands felt while he stretched out to give her complete access.

She decided to lick him several times to see how he tasted. He tasted good so she licked a few more times. He grabbed her hair, moaning louder and longer. She liked his response and decided to continue rubbing and licking then sucking to see if she could make him scream. He grabbed a pillow to muffle the sound of his yell, and after a minute pulled his penis out of her mouth so he could flip her around and return the favor. When his lips kissed her thighs, she moaned. When he licked her slowly in just the right spot between her legs, she had her first orgasm of the night. It was her turn to use the pillow to muffle the sound of her scream.

Finally, he pulled her up off the sofa and walked her over to one of the armchairs, asking her to bend over and hold on to the front of the arms of the chair, and look out the window.

"Now we can both see the moon and stars and city lights while we enjoy each other." He loved the way the light from outside created shadows in the apartment and on their bodies. It was sexy, stimulating, and he hoped she was enjoying it too.

He reached around her to caress her breasts with one hand and rub between her legs with the other as he found a steady rhythm to pump into her. He leaned over to whisper in her ear, telling her how good she felt and asking if what he was doing was making her feel good.

She moaned, "Mmm-hmm," and looked over her shoulder so she could see his face. She could tell from his expression, eyes closed in concentration, when he had found a spot inside her that he liked because he smiled and stayed there for a while, sliding in and out slowly, feeling every part of her. His hands all over her body and watching him enjoy her was so sexy she had to tell him, "Jeff. I love the way you feel inside me. You feel so good and are so sexy I could make love with you every day." He liked the sound of that and increased the force of pushing into her.

She started squeezing him with her muscles. She could feel them both ready to explode and braced herself. He slammed into her then pulled almost out then slammed into her again. And again. The pressure of her tightness and squeezing her muscles sent him over the edge. She was right there with him. "OOOHHHH! OOOHHHH!" was all they could say in unison.

When their breathing returned to normal, she stood up and turned to kiss him then slowly led them to the shower. Neither one said a word as they soaped each other and kissed.

They went to the kitchen for water and shared a chicken sandwich that she had bought when she came from the stylist but never ate. Dancing, wine, and sex made them hungry.

They got in the bed and assumed their usual position then pulled the covers up. They weren't sleepy so they started talking.

"Why aren't you married Jeff? You are so thoughtful and loving. And with Jimbo too? You would be a nice package for anyone to come home to."

He told her honestly, "I've been told that my sexual appetite is too much. I didn't think it was. I live in a very masculine world, physical labor, many decisions to make, trying to help guide Steven and Jason, so I like having the softness of a woman to offset all that testosterone. I like the physical contact of kissing, making love, and being together with someone special. I guess none of the women I've known since my divorce have been the right ones."

She snuggled closer and said, "Well I'm glad you're not married or with someone else. I like the way you love me. I'm looking forward to a lot more of this."

He whispered in her ear, "Me too. And maybe if I love on you right, and we're together long enough, one day you will love me back. I knew a week ago, and every day that we have been together I have grown more sure, that I want to be the only one you kiss and rub and lick and moan for." He was giving her the serious stare.

She was rubbing Jimbo as he talked so she stopped and looked up at him to say softly, "Jeff, we are very good together and I will probably get to where you are in my feelings. I just need you to wait a little longer than a week. Geez. I thought I was impatient."

They both laughed.

"I'm good with that V. I need to know that you want what I want. Just us. Together. Will you at least be okay with us being in a committed relationship?"

"That I can do for sure," she promised. "Good," he said. "Very, very good," as he dozed off. She smiled and settled in for the night, thinking as well, yes, very good indeed.

Chapter Fourteen

The next week was the adjustment period they needed to solidify their relationship. More and more of her clothes appeared at his house and remained there. He was happy to make room for her in the closets and in his life. She didn't change her routine, just did everything from his house.

On Wednesday, he came home early from work to take her to *POST Houston*. The old Barbara Jordan post office had been completely renovated and there were a variety of restaurants and and art installations to explore. The roof deck, Skylawn, provided a lovely city view and a balmy breeze that was relaxing. He was fascinated with how they had re-created the multi-level structure and she was a willing student, listening as he explained the changes to the building from an engineer's perspective.

They held hands and browsed the whole afternoon, stopping for a snack and then dinner before heading home. It was a full and fun date, leaving them each looking forward to more adventures together.

They agreed on Friday to go to the first of the four weeks of Salsa lessons they signed up for, and spend the night at her place afterwards. After the date, he gave her a massage on a blanket on the floor in the living room. There was something about the idea that people might be able to see them that was a turn on for them both even though they were far away from the next building. They joked about who might be looking through binoculars or a telescope.

"Some old man is watching us and remembering when he used to be able to do this," Jefferson decided.

"Or some young couple is using us as their X-rated movie, and they make up their own sound." Valerie giggled just imagining how they looked through someone else's eyes.

They had gone shopping for body oil. He insisted that it be flavored so he could taste it on her skin. She showed him how to warm the oil, making sure it wasn't too hot. His hands were a little rough but added to the pressure in the right places as he rubbed long, slow strokes all over her body. He added another dimension by licking her everywhere he rubbed. She finally understood exactly what people meant by "happy endings" at the massage parlors. She learned quickly that she could have an orgasm just from him kissing and rubbing on her.

When Jefferson and Valerie had been dating for just over a month, Valerie was invited to Jeannette's for the regular Ware family meeting. It was held every Saturday morning from ten until noon to keep everyone up to date on Jefferson's business. Valerie learned how Jeannette and Steven were Jefferson's check and balance for business dealings so he didn't miss an opportunity or when someone might have tried to steal from him. The assumption was that

Jeannette, then Steven, then Jason would inherit the business so the weekly meetings were necessary and included everybody.

It was Jeannette who brought up the elephant in the room. This was their fifth meeting since Jefferson and Valerie met even though it was Valerie's first time attending. Her presence made it clear that Valerie was going to be a big part of their lives. Jeannette looked at Jefferson when she asked, "So are you two getting married? If so, what happens to the business? Does it now all go to Valerie?" Her tone was questioning and her voice had a disapproving edge to it.

Valerie was caught off guard by the question. She was still not ready to say she loved Jefferson or that she would marry him so she never thought of the business as possibly being hers. She looked at Jefferson, waiting for him to answer his sister. Steven looked at his mother, curious about why she was even asking the question since it was his uncle's business to do whatever he wanted with it.

Jefferson said what Valerie was thinking. "Honestly Valerie and I have not talked about it. Until we do and she's ready to take that next step of being a part of this family, she is just an additional set of eyes on the business by someone who has a business background and a vested interest in me and can offer some perspective. When she says yes, then we will figure it out."

You could tell that this was not the answer Jeannette was hoping for. She wanted some assurance that the plans would not change so late in the game. She gave Valerie the family history so she would understand and back off.

"Jefferson, Steven, and I lived together in the first house Jefferson ever bought. We stayed in the house for a few years after I got my degree so I could save some money and eventually get our own place, the house I live in now.

"Jefferson got his real estate license then started building his portfolio of houses. It was my husband's lawn care business that he has now, which he bought from me. I have no money invested in any of the houses. My responsibility, outside of the Saturday meetings, is to make sure all the vacated houses are cleaned and repaired where needed, ready for the new tenants. That doesn't happen a lot because we tend to get long term renters.

"When it seemed that Jefferson would probably not get married or have kids, I assumed that because I helped build the business it would be a family legacy, passed to me, then my son and grandson. I also assumed Jefferson felt the same way. I believe that we should get it all, not some newcomer with no time invested." You could hear and feel the tension in her voice. It was definitely a sore spot for Jeannette. Valerie knew this might become a problem between the brother and sister, and eventually, between Jeannette and Valerie.

Jefferson looked closely at Jeannette and how anxious she was as she told their story. He realized that he was going to have to be very sensitive to her feelings. They never put formal documents of co-ownership or successor paperwork in place about the business, but she and Stevens's names were on all the bank accounts and Jeannette was his power of attorney for business so it was unspoken. With Valerie in the picture now, he would have to work with his attorney to figure how to divide the properties once he and Valerie got married.

On the way home later that day, Valerie and Jefferson were quiet, both thinking of the conversation. Valerie finally spoke up to offer her perspective and keep him from having to choose between providing for her and satisfying Jeannette. Or finding a hybrid that would probably never satisfy Jeannette no matter how little Valerie got or how much she learned to like Valerie.

"You know you mentioned marriage but we have not talked about it since it's only been a month that we have been together. We don't have to get married Jeff. I don't want to put that pressure on you or come between you and your family because of your business. I think that our living arrangement is fine as it is. I have my place and my own money, thanks in large part to my financial settlement, and you have yours because you are smart and tenacious. I'm good with that."

Just as she finished her statement, he pulled up to the house. He turned the car off and looked at her. "What if I'm not good with that? I've been thinking more and more of how much I enjoy you, how good we are together, and I want us to be married. I want you as my wife, to take care of you and provide for you. All I have is the business to do that with so there has to be a way for you to be taken care of and Jeannette can get her share to pass on. I'm going to work on that. You need to keep working on loving me. Or are you really saying you don't ever want to marry me so Jeannette can have it all?"

Jefferson was still hurting over being rejected by his ex, Alicia. He never acknowledged that the hurt was underneath all of his relationships after the divorce, which is probably the real reason why he never got married again. It was hard to be loving and caring then find out people didn't want you or your love. With Valerie, he finally took a real chance and now it felt like it was happening all over again.

"It's not that," Valerie tried to tell him. "I'm not saying that I wouldn't eventually want to marry you, but I can see that this is a huge deal. I just didn't want to be the one to make it a bad situation between you and your family."

He responded quietly, asking, "But can you say that you would want to marry me one day?"

"I want to be with you Jeff. Why can't that be enough for now?" To Valerie, it was still so early in their relationship that they didn't need to come to any hard conclusions yet.

He told her he had to make a run so she needed to get inside. It was a first. She offered to go with him but he said no.

"You said communication was important Jeff. Why can't we talk? I'm saying I want to be with you. I'm asking you to be patient about the marriage and you said ok. Are you not ok with waiting?"

He didn't answer her directly and didn't look at her, just asked her to go on in the house, he would be back.

She slowly got out of the car, asking him to please come inside.

"Don't leave me or us like this. Come on Jeff. When Helen came over, you wouldn't let me go home until we worked through it. Let's do it again to get through this."

He couldn't look at her. He couldn't see through his hurt. He could only feel rejection headed his way. He wanted to be alone. As soon as she closed the door, he started the car and took off.

He drove to Bush Intercontinental Airport and sat in the parking lot. His engineer mind was relaxed when around planes. He would think about times in the Air Force and in school when working on drawings or actual planes excited him. Watching planes take off and land kept him entertained for hours so he pushed his seat back and watched.

He thought about his ex-wife, Alicia, and the pain she put him through. They were together almost eight years and she never indicated that she was unhappy. When he would be off from one job, he would be at home with her, cooking, cleaning, and washing clothes so she never had to. She could focus on studying.

When he was off from both jobs, they would go out. She appreciated not having to work like some of her fellow students, and her loans were being paid off each term so she would not have any debt to start her practice.

Toward the end, the last year or so, he noticed she was quiet and didn't want to go out with him as much. She would be out more when he was working, and when he was home, she would be asleep most of the time. Alicia stayed with him until the day before her graduation. She took most of the money out of their bank accounts and moved all of her clothes and books to her new apartment while he was at work. He was served with divorce papers on his job.

The lesson he learned was that when women don't say yes, a no is coming, whether it's about where to go for dinner, kids, or getting married. Valerie's no to marriage was clear. He would respect that and not think about marrying her anymore. It was not what he wanted, but he couldn't see how their current living arrangement would work long-term. He wanted them to be married eventually and in one house together.

In the meantime, Valerie was pacing the floor and wondering if she was about to lose the best man she ever knew. Why couldn't she say she would marry him? Why was she making him wait? He had proven over and over again that he cared deeply for her and wanted to take care of her and make her happy.

He wanted to marry her, not just live with her, or continue the make-shift living arrangements they had now. He had been generous and patient even though it had just been a few weeks. She felt like a fool. She finally said it out loud, "I love him. I want to be with him, marry him, and have a happy, fun life. What is wrong with me that I can't tell him that?"

She knew the answer: not only is she still married, she never got over being rejected herself, traded in for another, slightly younger woman. Only Jeannette wasn't a lover. She was family, close family, and to the Wares, family always came first, winning out over everything and everybody.

Valerie didn't want Jefferson to have to choose. Even though he said he loved her and wanted to provide for her and he would figure out a way to make it all work out once she said yes to marrying him, she knew Jeannette would likely not be satisfied with anything short of having it all. She had put in the time and the work and she expected her reward, her legacy. Valerie firmly believed that was a pressure Jefferson should not have to bear.

She called Jefferson every half hour, begging him to please come home, getting his voice mail every time. After about four hours she stopped, packed her clothes and put them in her car, then sat in the den to wait for him. She thought about immediately going to her place and letting him have his space but she wanted to be there when he came home. She needed to see him and get this resolved. Then she would go back to her place, back to her home, and her life without Jefferson.

Chapter Fifteen

Jefferson walked in at almost seven the next morning, looking exhausted. She asked where he had been and why hadn't he answered any of her calls. He explained about being at the airport, realizing that she was probably thinking that he was with another woman. He did not offer the parking receipt as proof. She didn't want him, why should he be so transparent?

"I relax watching the planes. I turned my phone off so I could just be by myself." No apology, just facts. "I'm going to take a shower and get some sleep before game time." He walked away, not offering to talk about the conversation from the day before. When he walked into the bedroom, he knew immediately that she had cleared out all of her things. He was not surprised.

While he was in the shower, she left. She did not feel like family anymore and did not feel very social. She would not fake it.

When Jeannette came over and Jefferson explained that Valerie was gone, Jeannette said she was sorry for him, but inside she was gloating. She knew Valerie wanted what was rightly hers. Jeannette was glad it happened now and not after Jefferson married her.

Jefferson could not get into Game Day. He should have cancelled it. He stood at the door to the den and half watched the game, walking to the windows in the family room for periods at a time, missing Valerie. Everybody knew something was wrong.

Jeannette was standing her ground about the property and did not acknowledge his anxiety. Steven tried to talk to him about it, going into the family room to sit with him during half time, but Jefferson had nothing to say.

He had never seen his uncle like this. He wanted to be there for Jefferson the way Jefferson had been for him through the years.

Steven gave his perspective. "I wasn't around when you and your wife broke up so all I have ever known was cool, ladies' man Uncle Jeff. I know this is about the property and told mom that I thought she was wrong for putting pressure on you. As far as I'm concerned, you can do whatever you want with it. Your being happy is all that counts, and if you need the property to get or keep Ms. Valerie, or to make sure she's taken care of, and that's who you want, then do it."

Jefferson looked at him and shared his thoughts. "I appreciate your concern and advice. I will figure something out. I just don't know if Valerie will be around when I do." Game Day ended early.

Valerie and Jefferson tossed and turned all night, not getting any sleep. The problem was they were in their own homes alone, loving and missing each other.

Jefferson went to the flower shop the next day. He didn't know if they could work through this, but he knew they never would if they weren't face to face. He also knew that Valerie was protecting him and his family so he had to make the first move.

Fay informed him, "Valerie called this morning and said that she would not be in all week, she would catch up next week. She has never done this before Jefferson, and I'm worried about her." She thought to herself, since Jefferson was looking for her, and looking pretty haggard, she surmised that they must have had a fight. A big one.

He headed for Valerie's place. Since he had been introduced to the staff and become a regular in and out of the building, with and without Valerie, he had no problems getting to her door without the doorman at the desk calling her for permission to let him up. He had her key with him but didn't feel he had the right to use it for this visit. If the conversation didn't go well, he knew he would end up giving the key back.

He tapped lightly but she didn't respond. He kept tapping until she came to the door, irritated. She didn't even look through the peephole, just snatched the door open. When she saw who it was she looked at him for a minute then backed away from the door, not sure what to think. He stepped inside and closed the door as he wrapped his arms around her for a hug. He walked her over to the sofa and sat her in his lap.

VALENTINE LOVE

"Why can't you love me V? I thought we were having such a good time and getting so close." He buried his head in her neck, so glad to see her and hold her.

"That's just it." She lifted his head to look into his eyes and finally confessed. "I do love you. I figured out that I started falling in love with you the day you walked into the flower shop. Between the flowers on Thursday, the food on Valentine's Day, lunch on Saturday, and every day ever since, I have been falling for you. You are a hard man not to love. You are fun, funny, so damn sexy, smart, and loving, you give me just the kind of love I want."

"Then how did we get here? Over some property? You packed up everything and left me. I'm miserable, I think you missed me too since you didn't go to work and are hiding out. What is it?"

"It's not about the property Jeff. I don't want to put you in an uncomfortable position of having to choose me over your family. So when I think about marrying you, the man who excites me every moment of every day, who knows me and loves me like I am the Queen of his universe, nothing would make me happier. For the sake of peace, however, I would rather we just keep things like they are. You disagree. So much so that you left me all night. See what this is doing to us already?

"The other problem is Jeannette doesn't trust me, so when I say I don't care about the property, she will never believe me or let you rest about it. You don't need that headache. I know family comes first for the Wares."

She took a breath before continuing. "It's better for me to just get through this separation and stay by myself. Therefore, Mr. Jefferson Ware, know that I love you so much, but I don't want to come between you and your family, especially something you guys have built together. I know you and the way you love me. You would make sure I had a sizeable share of the property because as your wife you would provide for me that way." He nodded his head, agreeing with her about the property.

"So let me get this straight. You love me?" he asked, looking at her with a questioning look. "You really love me? Valerie Mason loves Jefferson Ware? Like in the forever and ever till death do we part kind of love?" They both started laughing and she rolled her eyes.

"Yes Jeffy. Mommy loves you. This much." She made her voice sound like a mother talking to her five year old little boy, reminding him of the second day she was at his house and he thought she did not come to stay with him for the week.

She opened her arms wide and wrapped them around his shoulders. He responded sounding tough. "You can call me Jeffy, Jiggly Wiggly, or any other name you can think of to tease me. One thing is for sure: I love the hell out of you woman, and one day we are getting married. I'm not asking anymore and you are never leaving me alone again, unless you are hanging out with your girlfriends on vacation somewhere. And that better not be too often."

She was curious. "Wait. Before we get to the altar, you left me at the house for the night so tell me why you were so upset, especially when you said you would work out the property stuff without either me or Jeannette getting involved."

He got serious again and sighed. "I had flashbacks to the hurt after my marriage ended. She never told me that she didn't want me anymore until she was done with medical school and all the bills were paid in full. All of a sudden, I'm not good enough. I wasn't man enough or classy enough for her. My love was not what she wanted in her life. I was crushed and felt used.

"A lifetime later, the first woman I truly feel something special for, and I can't get you to love me no matter how hard I love you or try to get you to love me. Then you would let some talk about property come between us? Talk about low self-esteem! I can see why men are labeled as dogs when they play on women's feelings. After you, that was going to be my way of life. No more love for me. It hurts too much.

"And now I find out you've been holding out on me, loving me but willing to leave just to be considerate. I love you for being so thoughtful, but we can't let family or the business come between us ever again."

"What about Jeannette?" Valerie knew that she would be a big hurdle to climb.

"I will figure out the property division and you and Jeannette will both learn to live with it. She will come around. She loves her big brother and she knows I will always take care of my family. That doesn't mean everybody always gets what they want or as much as they think they deserve." They both got quiet for a moment, just enjoying looking at each other. Then Valerie heaved a heavy sigh and moved off his lap. She stayed on the sofa with him but moved a couple of seats over and turned to face him.

"Okay. Now that we are clear on the Ware family, there is something you need to know about the Mason family."

Chapter Sixteen

Jefferson had a feeling this was not going to be good news. He had a guarded look on his face. "What is it? Just say it."

Valerie took a deep breath and looked him in his eyes when she said, "My divorce is not final."

"Because…?" he asked. He wondered if she was about to tell him they were trying to work things out. If that was the case, he wondered, why had she been at his house for the last month?

She gave him the details. "It's been over two years since I put Vincent out. We had just resolved the financial division in court the week before you and I met. Initially that was a fight because he wanted to hold the money over my head to keep us from divorcing. I think his lawyer saw that I was not interested in staying married and talked to Vincent because eventually he did what was right since he had cheated.

"I got the house we were living in and sold it to buy my condo. He bought a house in River Oaks. I get over half of both the investments and his retirement since he was the cheater. There were no issues with Nikki because she is an adult. I just requested that she become the beneficiary for his home and insurance policies and everything else so none of his lady friends could try to get his money that my daughter should have."

"So why aren't the papers signed? Are you two trying to work things out? Are you thinking about getting back together with him?" Jefferson was anxious to know if he was just a test for her to help her decide if she really did want her husband back. Maybe this was the real reason why she did not respond when he first asked her to stay for the week, and why she could not say yes to marrying him.

"I do not want him back." She looked in Jefferson's face and saw that he still had his guard up. She took his head in her hands and looked directly in his eyes, repeating what she had just said. "I definitely do not want him back. Apparently, he and his sidepiece broke up. He decided he wanted us to go to counseling to see if I would forgive him and take him back. It's not court mandated. I said yes just to see if I could learn something about why he cheated and get him to sign the papers faster.

"I never pushed to get it done once we lived separately because I didn't have anyone I wanted to marry. Until now. Nothing has changed for me but he keeps begging for us to try again, saying that I am still hurt and need more time to reconsider the divorce. We go back to court in May. This is the last possible delay so the divorce should be final by the end of June, once all the final paperwork is processed."

"I see. So what happens until then? More counseling? Are you dating?" Jefferson didn't mind competition, but how could he win against a thirty-year marriage? Women often forgive men, especially husbands, for infidelity.

"No, not dating. Counseling is scheduled, every couple of weeks. It was recommended that we talk outside of the counseling sessions so he calls a couple of times a week. Vincent wants us to have lunch or dinner to have time to talk but I'm not interested in any of that. I went to the first counseling session and told the therapist it would not help me change my mind. I am not going back. I ignore Vincent's calls and we have missed the last couple of the sessions. He's a bit frustrated based on the messages he leaves so who knows what he will do."

Suddenly the air felt thick and Jefferson wanted to get clarity before he could think about this news. "Okay. Thanks for telling me. So what does that mean for us?"

Valerie put a smile on her face and tried to give him a happy response. "It means we keep moving forward, being together in your house and here on date nights, kissing and making love until the divorce is final. Then we get married." She decided to put her desires out there. She could tell Jefferson was hesitant to believe her and she understood. Her separation from Vincent was not that long ago and the longer it took to get the divorce, the harder it would be to convince Jefferson that she wanted them to get married.

Jefferson nodded his head, trying to figure out what to believe. He felt like she loved him and in the last month he had no signs that Vincent was an issue. Her phone rang a lot at night sometimes but she always checked caller id to see if it was Nikki or her sister then sent the calls to voicemail. He thought she was doing it so as not to interfere with their time together. Now he knew the real reason why.

"I really do want to be with you Jeff. One day I want to be married to you. I have to get out of this marriage first before I can even begin to think about another." She looked at him and he looked out of her window, wondering for the first time if he should believe her.

"I hope so V. I guess we will know in the next few weeks if that is still true. I was hoping we would be married by the end of the year." He went to the kitchen for a beer, processing this new development and deciding to proceed with caution. Once he had a handle on Vincent's game plan, he would create his own. In the meantime, he would enjoy the evening with the woman they both apparently love.

Valerie stayed in the living room, thinking of how to get rid of Vincent before she lost her chance with Jefferson. Vincent was being more aggressive in his efforts to get her back. She knew she needed to finalize the divorce if she and Jefferson were going to have a real chance.

When he came back from the kitchen, Jefferson sat on the sofa. He nodded his head to get her to lay across him in his lap so he could rub her back and legs then announced, "I love you V. And I will fight for you if you promise to always be honest with me and keep reminding me that you really want to be with me."

This time Valerie gave him the 'Ware stare.' Finally, she smiled and said, "I do. Indeed I do. We will fight Vincent Mason together. Team Ware. Deal?"

"Deal. Okay, now that that is settled, what do you want to do tonight?" Jefferson wanted desperately to change the subject. He did not want to think of Vincent Mason or the possibility that Valerie might go back to him another minute.

"Will you stay here with me? I don't want to go back to the real world just yet." Valerie felt they needed this time together.

"I will stay wherever you want me." He needed to be close to her, better yet inside her, to be comforted by her body and feel confident that she was really his so he offered, "How about we shower together and see if anyone is up tonight to watch while we get naked and me and Jimbo try to make you scream?" She felt her face flush and wondered if she would ever stop reacting to the bold or risqué stuff that he says.

"Sounds good to me." She jumped up and raced him to the bathroom, happy to be happy again.

Chapter Seventeen

Life was back on track. Valerie and Jefferson decided to spend the week together since she had called off work anyway. He didn't have any big projects so he let Ron handle all the jobs.

They drove to San Antonio for a few days, staying at a bed and breakfast. It sounded like a good idea at the time, but when they got there and saw that the rooms were close together, they realized it was going to be hard to make love since both of them were so noisy. They decided to use the pillows like they do at her place to help muffle most of the sound. It actually felt sexy to feel like they had to sneak.

The weather was perfect—sunny and not too warm, so they took advantage of all the outdoor activities: walking along the River Walk, stopping to eat when the mood struck them, trying different Mexican foods and drinks, and walking around the shops and restaurants in the Pearl Brewery District. Since they both love art and wine, they went to the McNay Art Museum, then drove seventy miles to Fredericksburg to visit a couple of wineries.

Everyone called her Mrs. Ware and she liked the sound of it, as well as the feel of it on her own tongue. Jefferson was over the moon that they were back together and he wanted to buy her a gift to commemorate their renewed commitment and their trip. Every time they passed a jewelry store, they looked for just the right thing, and they found it the last day before returning to Houston.

It was a four-carat Emerald cut black diamond ring set in platinum, a sign of his love for her until they were free to get married. She would wear it on her left hand until the wedding ceremony then switch it to her right hand because she didn't want a traditional diamond wedding set when they got married. Been there done that.

She wanted something totally different with Jefferson, and they found wedding bands that looked great on both of their hands. Valerie was a little superstitious about getting too far ahead of themselves and something go wrong so she insisted he not buy them yet and wait until her divorce was final. The jeweler took their ring sizes and made note of their selection. Jefferson made sure to take the jewelers card.

Once they returned to Houston, they spent the rest of the week secluded at his house. They talked about how they could incorporate her furnishings into his house once they got married or if they would need to find a larger place.

They both agreed they liked his house because it was large enough yet felt cozy and had a lot of light, plus it was in a great neighborhood. Since no other woman had lived there with Jefferson, Valerie had no issues with moving into it.

She suggested, "Why don't we keep the condo for our date nights, and for Nikki and any family visitors? That way, we can leave the furnishings right where they are?"

He was initially okay with the idea, but shared his concern. "I don't want you to feel like you don't belong because there is nothing of yours in the house."

"I will have you, all my clothes, and I'll bring over a few keepsakes so that will be enough. You have put together a great home. I'm just happy to be able to share it with you. My furnishings are pretty new so none of it has any special meaning or value for me."

They discussed a wedding date. Jefferson reminded her that he wanted it to be before the year was out, as soon as her divorce was final. To Valerie, any date was fine as long as Nikki could be there, and hopefully, her sister Stephanie.

He asked about the wedding. "Alicia and I didn't have one. We went to the courthouse to save money." Valerie reminded him about her destination wedding the first time around. This time she wanted it simple too. "Just the two of us; Nikki; Stephanie; Jeannette, Steven, Jason, and Ann; Lillian and Max; Fay and her husband, Rick; and Reyna and Billy because they are like family and helped kick-start our relationship with your grand flower gesture. Anyone else you want to include?"

His male friends were happy for him but had no desire to attend a wedding. He reminded her, "I don't care as long as you are there. Whatever you want."

She had girlfriends and family in town and in other cities but knew that would make it big so she decided not to tell any of them.

The ceremony would definitely be in a church chapel and afterwards they all would go to a very nice restaurant for a private lunch.

Valerie and Jefferson had traveled abroad extensively in their lives and wanted to re-visit some of the same places they had been. Seeing some of their favorite places with older eyes and a different companion would give them a fresh perspective.

"I'll take care of all of the honeymoon arrangements," Jefferson announced, "and you can have whatever wedding you want." He ordered a platinum AMEX card in the name of Valerie Ware for her to use for whatever expenses she would incur.

Valerie went back to work the next week. She told Fay she had taken off to take care of some business. She was not interested in sharing the details of what had happened in her relationship, even with her favorite cousin. Fay figured from the sound of her voice when she called off initially that they were heart things she had to take care of so she was glad to see the smile on Valerie's face and the ring on her finger when she came back.

When Valerie told Lillian and Nikki that she was going to marry Jefferson, they were both happy. She never told Lillian about what Jefferson called their "moment of misunderstanding." She had not had time to process it all for herself so she never had a sobbing, "oh woe is me" call with her friend which kept Lillian still happy for her. Lillian was especially happy because she liked Jefferson and predicted this would happen.

Nikki was surprised and encouraging. She wanted her mother happy so she scheduled a visit to meet Mr. Wonderful who had her mother's heart, soul, and life in his hands. Memorial Day was coming up in a couple of weeks so she booked a flight with plans to stay for the long week-end.

Valerie went into mother mode, making sure the apartment was clean and the pantry stocked with Nikki's favorite food, drinks, and snacks. She didn't even care when the May court date was pushed back because Vincent and his lawyer were both scheduled to be out of town. August twentieth was the final court date according to the judge, with or without Mr. Mason in the courtroom. Valerie was going to enjoy seeing Nikki and would wrestle with Vincent and her attorney after Nikki left.

Jefferson was amused as he watched Valerie's excitement build and appreciated that she had so much love for the people she cared about. He was glad to be one of them. His thoughts turned to his sister and how he could get her to see this loving side of Valerie. It was time to tell her that he and Valerie were definitely getting married, and to prepare for a hailstorm of anger. He knew he could not tell Jeannette in front of Valerie so he stopped by her house one evening after work instead of waiting for the Saturday meeting.

"This is a surprise," Jeannette said when she opened the door. She was instantly on guard. Her brother didn't just drop by unless something was up. He sat down and got right to the announcement.

"Valerie has agreed to marry me." He paused to see what response he would get. There was none. No congratulations, no "I already figured that," no nasty comment. Just silence and a 'Ware stare.'

Finally she said, "And?"

"And I need you to get on board with her being in our family. My wife. I need the two most important women in my world to get along. You are harboring some ill will about who will get the business and not trying to get to know Valerie as a person. She is kind, loving, and smart. She loves her daughter like you love Steven and Jason. Both of you are financially independent. You might have even more in common but you don't try to find out. She was willing for us to break up to keep you happy and you are barely civil to her. I don't know why you are so suspicious of her. It's not like you even need the money or would really want the responsibility. Most of that would probably fall on Steven.

"I will make the decision on the business without you or Valerie. I know what you want and I know what I want to do for Valerie and you have to let me take care of my family the way I see fit. *ALL* of my family. Let me handle the business while you make more of an effort to get to know her. For me. Please."

This was the first time Jeannette and Jefferson had ever had a major difference of opinion and it was unsettling for both of them. Jeannette finally promised, "I'll see what I can do." Jefferson was disappointed that she wasn't happy for him and she could see it on his face. He left, deciding that the ball was in her court and he would be hopeful that she would come around. He was marrying Valerie regardless, but he wanted his sister to be happy for him.

Jeannette was hurt, almost like a jilted love. She was happy that her brother had someone special, but if Valerie was so financially stable, why did he have to marry her? They were already living together. Wasn't that enough at their ages? Why did he feel the need to give her any part of the business—taking money away from his blood, the ones who had his back all these years?

Jeannette already knew it would take time for her to get over the issue of dividing the business, if she ever did. She promised herself to start with not being antagonistic when she and Valerie were in the same space. Then maybe she could begin to be civil. Baby steps.

Chapter Eighteen

The Memorial Day holiday weekend finally arrived and Jefferson and Valerie headed to Hobby Airport to pick up Nikki and Checkers. When Jefferson saw her, he could see how much like her mother she looked. She was tall like Valerie, with milk chocolate brown skin, very interesting, almost exotic eyes, and thick black hair cut in a short tapered natural style. A very pretty young lady.

Nikki greeted her mother with a big hug and lots of kisses, then took a few minutes to look her over to, as she said to her mother, laughing, "Let me see how you look in love with this new man." Jefferson immediately thought that Steven would like her. Although Ann, Jason's godmother, lived with Steven and Jason and was around the family since before Jason was born, Jefferson had a feeling that she and Steven did not have more than a brother/sister relationship. Steven had yet to date again since his wife died, but Jefferson didn't think that Ann was his type. She was attractive and nice but quiet around the family, not as pretty or as bubbly as Carla, Steven's wife had been, or Nikki seemed to be, based on his first impression. That was more Steven's type.

Valerie and Nikki talked quietly while Jefferson put her bags and the dog in the car. Valerie reaffirmed to her that she indeed loved Jefferson and would marry him as soon as she could get free from Vincent and Nikki could come back.

Then Nikki turned to Jefferson with a somber look on her face. She looked him up and down and walked all around him before giving him a big grin and hug, saying, "Thank you for making my mother so happy. Please do not hurt her. My daddy did enough to last her a lifetime."

He promised her on his life that he would not hurt her mother. She looked him in his eyes to make sure he was serious. She believed the saying that the eyes were the window to the soul and could always tell when people were lying or did not have good character by the shifty way their eyes moved or they would not look at you. He looked directly back at her with all sincerity.

"So what do I call you? I'm too old for Mr. Ware, or Mr. Jefferson or Mr. Jeff, even though I know it's the polite way for us southern folks to show respect. Let's see…you're going to be around for a long time so it's got to be something we can both enjoy. I'll have to think of something that fits over the week-end as I get to know you."

They all laughed, and he said whatever she was comfortable with was fine with him. They were off to a good start and settled into the car, heading for Jefferson's house. Valerie was happy that they seemed to have a good introduction.

Since Valerie was basically living with Jefferson, and Nikki would be with them most of the week-end, they discussed the logistics of her staying with them versus at the condo, even though Valerie had prepared it for her. Nikki could take Valerie's car wherever she wanted to go, Valerie would drive Jeff's Mercedes if she needed to go somewhere, and Checkers would have a nice backyard to play in.

Once Nikki saw the house and heard about family Game Day, she was happy to stay in one of the guest rooms. She wanted to get to know Jefferson's family since it was going to be her family too.

With all of the excitement, Valerie and Jefferson had ordered food for dinner so they ate as soon as they got to the house. They all talked for a while in the kitchen and helped Checkers get to know his new surroundings. He was a good dog, and Jefferson got on the floor in the den to play with him and make him comfortable. Nikki went to bed early since she had such an early flight and long day.

Valerie and Jefferson assessed the meeting and discussion. "I think all went well don't you?" She wanted his take before getting too happy. She would probably not want to get married unless and until Nikki and Jefferson got along.

He was happy to tell her that he agreed. "I can see she is just like her mother so she will not be hard to love as a daughter. I just don't want her to be upset that you and her father will not be getting back together."

Valerie assured him that he had *nothing* to worry about. "Once I get the divorce decree, we can move forward with our plans. Vincent will never be in my life again if I have a say in the matter, except for things that involve our daughter."

Nikki and Jefferson were up early the next morning, drinking coffee, feeding Checkers, and talking when Valerie walked into the kitchen. She walked over to him for their usual morning kiss and he pulled back from her, embarrassed in front of Nikki. He had not been around a woman's adult child like this, so he wasn't sure what was appropriate.

Valerie laughed, saying that Nikki was a big girl and mature enough to handle their morning and evening greeting. She added, "She didn't see me and her father do this too often so it might be a bit of a shock. But she'll get used to it."

Nikki teased them, saying, "Didn't you two just get out of the same bed? And that wasn't enough?" She was shaking her head in mock disbelief. "This must be love. Let's just keep it to a kiss and I'll be okay. I don't want to be traumatized thinking of what else you two do. Yuck."

Jefferson laughed saying, "Oh boy, she speaks her mind too. Already acting like a Ware. She will fit right in."

Nikki had planned to spend the day with her dad so she asked her mother how much he already knew about the wedding plans.

"I don't talk to your dad about my life and I don't see any need to inform him about what I do. If he wants to know where you are staying, tell him it's with me. That's enough. As far as I'm concerned, that's all he needs to know and only because it's about you." Valerie didn't really care if he knew, but felt that Nikki didn't need to become his informant.

Jefferson watched Valerie's face as she talked about her ex, trying to determine if there were any feelings still left for him. He could not detect any but decided to ask after Nikki left.

"I appreciate him for being a good provider and father for Nikki, and for being generous in the financial settlement to keep it from being contentious. I will always be civil to him because of those two things. I talk to his brother Victor who lives in LA from time to time. He calls to check on me and fill me in on his California living. His sister Viveca lives in Dallas. I talk to her a couple of times a year for our birthdays."

It occurred to her that he might be asking because he was wondering what would happen if Vincent came back into the picture. Ex's often do that when they wake up and realize what a good thing they gave up for the new and different who turns out to be not quite what they thought or what they wanted.

On the other hand, maybe Jefferson was the jealous type. He never had a reason to be in the few months they had been together so she wasn't sure what he would be like if someone tried to talk to her.

"What are you thinking Jeff? That I might still want him even though I said I was already bored and done with him before he cheated? That a little time away has made me realize what a good man I lost? That would be a no and a hell no."

He nodded and smiled, glad to hear that confirmation.

Valerie decided to ask, "Are you a jealous man Jefferson? What would you do if someone tried to talk to me or you thought I might want someone else?"

He frowned and clutched his heart saying, "Don't even go there. I am as jealous as any other man who loves and wants to keep his woman. I would fight for you of course. But I'm also a realist. Learned that in my first marriage. If you don't want me anymore, there is nothing I can do to stop the train wreck to our relationship. I would prefer that you be happy so I would let you go.

"What about you V? Are you the jealous type when you love someone and are not bored with them? You were ready to walk out when Helen came by and she was not anybody I was in a relationship with. Is that what you do…just walk? Would you walk away without a fight? You wouldn't fight for me?"

Valerie looked at him closely before responding. "If she is coming on to you, you had better get her straight immediately. If she is someone you want, then like I said before, talk to me, tell me. If we can't work it out then I will move on to the next man who deserves me. But first, just so you know Mr. Ware, Jimbo will be going with me, and I will cut your eyes out so you had better make sure she likes your seeing eye dog."

Checkers came into the kitchen for water just at that time so they both laughed. Jefferson pulled Valerie into his arms and assured her that she and he and Jimbo were a package deal until death so he was not worried.

Chapter Nineteen

Sunday. Game day. Jeannette was still wary of Valerie's intentions but Jefferson told her to let it go or he would do just what she was thinking and leave Valerie most, if not all, of the property. He was a man of his word so Jeannette had to shift her attitude. She promised to try being friendly with Valerie again, but in her heart, until she knew what was going to happen with the business, she was just going to be cordial.

Nikki had spent the night with her dad so she came back to Jefferson's after Jeannette, Steven, Jason, and Ann had arrived. Jason was already playing with Checkers and asking if the dog was Uncle Jeff's present for him.

Jefferson and Valerie were in the kitchen getting the food set up so Jeannette let Nikki in.

You could hear Nikki was excited by the way she greeted Jeannette. "Hi new Auntie! I'm glad to meet you." They hugged and Jeannette led her to the family room and introduced her to Jason and Ann, explaining Ann's role in their lives. Nikki hugged Ann and told her, "It's so cool the way you stepped in to take care of Jason. That is a godmother's role as I understand it, but it sounds like you have gone above and beyond. I admire you for that." Jeannette told Nikki, "My son Steven, Jason's dad, is here somewhere."

Seeing how Jason had instantly fallen in love with Checkers, she sat on the floor and was talking to him and playing with Checkers too when Steven walked in the room.

Steven saw her first, how pretty she was with beautiful smooth brown skin, thick natural hair, the dreamiest eyes he had ever seen, and full, sexy lips. She was slender with long, long legs that he envisioned wrapped around him. He had not had a sexual thought like that since before Carla gave birth and it surprised him. He also noticed how nice and motherly she was talking to Jason and was immediately smitten with Nikki. He didn't say a word, just stared at her. Both Ann and Jeannette noticed too, looking at each other, then at him.

When Nikki looked up, she got that same awestruck look at Steven. Nikki finally spoke, very slowly and quietly. "You must be Steven. Jason looks like you. Good to meet you." She was sitting on the floor so she didn't get up to hug him as she had done with Jeannette and Ann, and shaking hands was too formal. It was an awkward moment.

Steven did not speak to her, and after a full minute of staring, finally spun around and went into the kitchen, looking for a break from the tenseness in the den.

Jeannette was right behind him, screaming the nickname his father had given him. "Deuce? Deuce?" Steven never stopped or turned around. When they got to the kitchen she asked, "What the hell is wrong with you?" She was trying to whisper but was enraged. "Why were you looking like that with Ann sitting right there?"

Valerie and Jefferson looked at each other and asked at the same time, "What happened?"

Steven sat at the table with his head down, not saying a word and not looking at anyone. Jeannette popped Steven on the head and proceeded to fill them in.

"Your nephew is in there looking at Nikki like…like he just saw Jesus himself, like he is dying of thirst and she is a gallon of water. All of a sudden he can't talk, just stares at her. Ann is watching this whole thing. I know her feelings are hurt." She popped Steven again, this time on the shoulder. "What is wrong with you?"

Steven looked up at Jefferson and Valerie and stuttered. "I…she…Oh God. I'm sorry."

Jefferson was nervous, not sure of what had happened and almost afraid to ask but he did and in a stern, fatherly voice. "What are you sorry for? What did you do?"

"I didn't do anything. I couldn't do or say anything so I came right in here." Steven was shaking his head.

"So what's the problem?" Jefferson asked, looking at Jeannette then back to Steven.

Steven explained with wonder and shock in his voice. "When I walked in the den and saw her and how beautiful she is, and the way she was talking to Jason, I got this feeling that I haven't had since Carla. It is crazy. It feels crazy and right now, it sounds crazy. She made me feel something, like I am alive again and not just going through life to take care of my son. Like I could scoop her up and take her home and we would live happily ever after. Like I want a family again. A wife. Her."

They heard the front door slam. Jeannette and Valerie headed to the den to find Nikki still with Jason but not talking, a sheepish look on her face. Ann was gone. Jeannette ran out the front door to try to catch her.

Chapter Twenty

Valerie sat down in the den to talk to Nikki. "What's going on Nikki? What happened?" They were close and Nikki knew she could talk to her mom about anything.

Nikki was shaking her head, still in disbelief at what had just happened. "Mom, I didn't do anything. I was talking to Jason about Checkers when *he* walked in. Steven. When I looked up he was staring at me and I saw this fine brother that I couldn't take my eyes off of. All I could think was that *I could have his babies*. Mom! I have never, ever thought that before about any man! None! Ever before! Holy cow." She got quiet again, still surprised at what had transpired.

She continued. "I said hello, but he didn't speak. He just stared then walked out. I heard Ann crying and when I looked at her, she was getting her purse to leave. I tried to stop her, but she said she had to go, that she had been in love with Steven for years and he never looked at her liked that. She said she couldn't stay and watch what might happen next."

It was Valerie's turn to shake her head. She had a feeling that something was going on between Ann and Steven but no one ever said what and she had not asked. What she did know, from talking with Jefferson, was that Ann had been there for Steven since day one of Jason's birth when his wife Carla died right in the hospital the same day. Steven and Ann never held hands or kissed or even looked at each other in a loving way in front of the family so you could not tell that they were anything but friends. Except Ann clearly wanted more. The question was whether Steven knew, and whether he wanted more with her, or had been leading her on to think that there could be more.

Valerie's next thought was what Jefferson and Jeannette would think about all of this. Especially whether Jeannette would have a problem if the kids started a relationship. She already had a problem with Valerie. This could make her believe that the Mason women were after all of their money and that was just not true. Time to get Steven's side.

Nikki stayed in the den while Valerie went back to the kitchen.

Jefferson and Steven were quiet when Valerie walked in and Jeannette came back in the house from talking with Ann. Jeannette was grumbling, "Oh my God. This is a mess." She asked Steven, "Did you know that Ann is in love with you? Has been for years? Wants to marry you and make a real family for Jason? That she wants to have a child with you?"

Steven looked guilty so they all knew that he knew. He confessed. "She told me a while ago that she loved me and wanted us to date and see if we could have a relationship. I have always told her that I was not ready for that and because of her relationship with Carla, I saw her as a sister, not someone I would love in an intimate way.

"I've been trying to ease her out of the day-to-day of our lives since Jason is in school now but it's hard. I can't pick him up after school because of work and she is the only "mother" or caregiver of any kind other than you two that he knows.

"Since I never had anyone I was interested in, I didn't push it. But now…I see now that was a mistake. I should have been better prepared for a day like today. Veronica Mason has just swept into my life and caused a firestorm in my heart and a few other places." He paused when he realized what he had just said and apologized. "I'm sorry, that was inappropriate. But true."

Jeannette was conflicted. She loved Ann like a daughter and really appreciated how she helped raise Jason so she was upset for her. Yet she also knew her son had been hurting and lonely for a long time. Above all, she wanted him and Jason to be happy. Nikki was leaving tomorrow so if they could just get through today maybe all of this would blow over before she came back for another visit.

Jefferson and Valerie wanted to wait until the house was clear of all family to talk. That would give them both time to figure out what to think or do.

Steven decided he needed to talk to Ann about their relationship and situation. If he didn't see Nikki for a while after today he could sort through his feelings. He slowly walked back into the den and that awestruck feeling enveloped him again. She felt it too. They looked at each other and half smiled with a question in both of their eyes – what now?

He sat on the sofa next to her and started talking. "Hi. Sorry about what happened earlier. I was caught off guard. I didn't expect…you." He didn't have to explain. She nodded that she understood.

"I'm going to go home now. I need to figure out what this means for me and my life, and I need to talk to Ann." He looked at her closely so he could remember her face. "I know I'll see you again, maybe not until the wedding which will give me time to figure things out. Are you okay with that?"

She nodded and said, "I don't want to come between you and Ann. You have established a long-term relationship with her so do what is right. We will get past this."

He replied quickly, "That's just it. I don't know that I want to get past it. But let me work on my life and the next time I see you we will talk." He gave her a long look and she nodded back at him, at a loss for words.

Steven went back to the kitchen to ask if Jason could stay with either his mom or Jefferson and Valerie so he would have time to talk with Ann. Jefferson and Valerie volunteered to give Jason more time with Checkers since he was having so much fun. Monday was a holiday so they didn't have to consider getting him to school. They would bring him home after they dropped Nikki and Checkers at the airport.

Secretly, Valerie was thinking that it would also give Nikki more time with Jason too. It might help her think about the level of responsibility she could end up with if she and Steven were to try to have a relationship.

Steven spoke with Jason about the fact that he was staying the night. "How would you like to spend the night with Uncle Jeff and Ms. Valerie and Ms. Nikki?"

"Are you staying here too?" Jason was comfortable staying with his Uncle Jeff so there was usually not an issue, but he noticed his grandmother *and* godmother had left so he was nervous.

"No, I'm going home. I see you are having fun with Checkers and he is leaving tomorrow so I thought you would want to stay here and play with him some more. I'll see you after Ms. Nikki and Checkers leave tomorrow. You can ride to the airport with them then come home."

"Where did godmommy go? Is she mad at me? Did I do something wrong?"

"No little man. Of course not. She saw you having so much fun with Checkers that she decided to skip Game Day and go have her own fun." Steven was hoping that Jason had not seen all that had transpired with Ann and Jeannette.

"Oh. Okay. See you tomorrow then." Jason was happy to continue watching his favorite cartoon and explaining what was happening on the screen to Checkers.

After Steven left, Jeannette, Jefferson, and Valerie filed into the den to speak with Nikki. She was deep in thought and startled when they walked in. Jason was busy with Checkers so they could talk, even if it had to be in a little code.

"Hey Nikki," Jeannette opened the conversation. "What's going on with you two?"

"Nothing." She looked at each of them individually. She was not ashamed or embarrassed about what had happened. They were all adults and she had learned early in life to deal with issues in a forthright manner. "There is definitely an attraction, but he already has a lot going on in his life. I do not break up homes. I know firsthand what that does to people. I will not have that on my conscience. We did not exchange numbers and we agreed to talk the next time I see him which will probably be at the wedding. This chapter has ended."

Jeannette appreciated Nikki's comments since she had seen everything firsthand with her own eyes. She shared with Valerie and Nikki, "I learned a long time ago that you don't always control who you are attracted to or love or who loves you. It was like that with my husband, Steven Sr." She took a moment to flash back in her mind to their relationship. He was the love of her life, so she told Valerie and Nikki the story.

"I met Steven's father the summer right after we graduated high school and were about to start our "adult" lives. He had a landscaping business that he had started in junior high. The Ware family house became one of his clients.

"For the first two weeks we just looked at each other when he came to cut the grass. We were attracted to each other but he saw us as middle class and he was from the poor side of town. He never believed he was from the right background for my family to let us date. But he liked talking to me and I liked talking to him. He finally asked me out. My parents said yes because he had proven to be a gentleman, was always on time, and never overcharged. They weren't the stuck up kind of people who would say their daughter couldn't date the guy who cut the grass."

Jeannette got quiet for a moment then finished the story. "I was headed to college at Florida A&M University with scholarships for a degree in chemistry. Steven was taking business classes at the junior college and trying to grow his business. We talked every night while I was away and we were together every day when I came home for holidays and breaks. He even visited me a couple of times on campus. I didn't last but one year before I came home, lovesick and refusing to live without Steven. We got married, and within a year, I was pregnant. Unfortunately he died a couple of years later."

Jeannette announced to Jefferson and Valerie that it was time for her to go home. "I want to be available in case Deuce needs to talk to me."

After Jeannette left, Valerie asked Jefferson, "Where did the name "Deuce" come from?" He explained. "Deuce is the nickname Steven's dad gave him when he was born. He was named after his dad, Steven Carter Jackson, but his dad hated to call him Junior so he called him Deuce. The family called him that until it was time for him to go to school and tell people his government name. Then Jeannette made us all start calling him Steven. When Jeannette gets in her feelings and is the protective mom, she still calls him Deuce. I think she is channeling her husband and hoping he will help her get through whatever is going on with their son."

As a mom, Valerie completely understood and had a lot of empathy for Jeannette. In the meantime, though, they were all anxious to see how things moved forward with Steven and Nikki.

Chapter Twenty-One

Nikki wanted to go to her room and pack but Jason had questions: "Why did you name him Checkers? How old is he? What are dog years? Where do you live? I've never seen you before. Are you staying for a long time? Where is Chicago? Can I come visit you and Checkers in Chicago? Why don't you and Checkers move here? When are you coming back?" She sat with him and answered every question, making sure to give him all of her attention.

When Jason went back to watching television, Nikki stayed with him with her thoughts fully on his father. She was serious about not breaking up a happy home so she did not want to get her hopes up too high. She was attracted to other men before, more than her fair share because she was a pretty girl with a fun personality so men often came on to her. She never thought, however, about having kids with any of them. This man was very different. She understood completely why her mom loved Jefferson. Steven had similar swagger and appeal: handsome, focused on you, thoughtful about his approach, direct. She bet he was smart and fun to be with too, and was clearly a great dad.

She also understood exactly why Carla wanted to have his baby, wondering if Steven would be interested in taking a chance on having a baby again. She didn't have any health issues, but knew that was going to be a big ask if they got together and started a relationship. She did ultimately want a family. Would he be interested in having one with her?

Valerie and Jefferson ate in the kitchen and put away what was left of the food. Jefferson finally broke the silence. "So it's not just you. All Mason women are a powerful force. Poor Steven. I know how he is feeling. Only I didn't have a child or an Ann in my life to consider. I was free to snatch you up." They both laughed.

"How would you feel if Steven and Nikki dated? Or even got married eventually?" Valerie wanted to make sure early on that he was not opposed to them having a relationship, especially since they would be family soon anyway. If that was going to be a problem, better to know it and deal with it now. She would also need to know from Jeannette too, but she would not have to ask. Jeannette would surely tell her the next time they were together.

"I want Steven to have someone good in his life and I want Jason to grow up with a mother's love. It is so critical for kids and he's already behind the curve with his mom being deceased.

"Plus I want Steven to be kind to Ann, especially if they need to change their arrangements. She's been great with Jason, even moved in with them to take care of the baby while Steven grieved and adapted to fatherhood then went back to work. Steven said she was sleeping in the guest room and he was paying her and she had free food and housing with him. If she was smart, she has most of her money saved or invested. There was a time I would have believed that she might have been great for Steven, but he is clearly not feeling her like that as the young folks say."

He continued. "If its Nikki he wants, then I want him to be sure that they are right together as a couple and separately, that Nikki is okay with being a mom to Jason for life. That is a lot on someone who has no children of her own. I don't count Checkers." He rolled his eyes.

Valerie wanted a temperature check. "So what do you think Jeannette will say?"

"I think she'll say what I am saying. We both just want the boys to be happy and not have a bunch of messy relationships in the process. What do you say Mother Valerie, with all the questions?"

"To be honest, I'm concerned. In the ideal world they fell in love today, Ann will find her own love, and they will all marry who they should marry and live happily ever after. But what if Steven and Nikki date and don't make it to marriage? They are still family because of us being together. That could be very awkward when she visits."

"They are both intelligent adults," Jefferson reminded her. "Let them work it out. In the meantime, let's get Nikki and spend this last day together in our own family circle."

They all converged in the den to watch a kid's movie with Jason. Nikki kept looking at him to see whether she could grow to love him like her own. He seemed drawn to her too, sitting on the sofa next to her and leaning on her as they watched the movie. Nikki could see even at five that he was going to be a heartbreaker in a few years. He had that direct look that seemed to be a trademark in the Ware family, and he loved to engage in conversation. Nikki could feel herself getting wrapped up in him and decided to call it an early night. She knew that if he was anything like his dad, Jason would capture her heart quickly. She needed to hold off on letting her feelings get too far ahead of the situation. This might be the turning point for Steven to finally say he loved Ann so she needed to be prepared.

The next morning Jefferson and Nikki had their morning coffee together and talked about his expectations. "As I told your mother already, I want Ann to be okay because she's a nice young lady and has invested a lot into Jason. It has helped Steven tremendously so he needs to be thoughtful about what happens next and be kind to her no matter what."

On that, they agreed. He continued. "And I want Jason to have a mother. If you are not prepared to be his mother for life, then do not start anything with Steven. Please. It will be enough if you love Jason as Aunt Nikki or Cousin Nikki or whatever you will be to him."

Nikki agreed to that too.

They dropped Nikki and Checkers off at the airport. She hugged them all and said she and Checkers had a great time. "I'm sorry to have interrupted family Game Day. Rest assured I will stay out of the way but will be thinking about everything while Steven decides what is best for him and Jason.

I'll see you all Labor Day week-end. Or sooner if you decide to come to Chicago." She was hinting with a smile.

"Oh, by the way, I have decided to call you Daddy J. Sometimes I might just call you Dad so don't be surprised. I like our morning coffee time together and the way you talk to me like a dad, even though I'm already an adult and have a father."

"I'm good with that," Jefferson responded with a grin and nodding his head. "I like that. Never been anybody's dad." He looked at Valerie and she was smiling at both of them. Life was good.

Valerie and Jefferson called Steven to make sure things were ok with him and Ann before they headed his way to bring Jason home. Steven said yes very quietly and with a heavy sigh. They could not talk details about what happened with Ann in the house so they dropped Jason off at home and went on home themselves.

Valerie decided to soak away some of the anxiety and tense energy from the weekend in a nice hot bath. Jefferson went to the den to relax and read. About an hour later, she was standing in the doorway of the den, not sure if he was awake or asleep. He was in his favorite position – sitting on the sofa facing the television, legs stretched out in front of him on the coffee table, his head laying on the pillow on the back of the sofa with his eyes closed. The book he was supposed to be reading was face down on his chest and his hands were on top of it.

He felt her presence and began to talk to her, not opening his eyes or turning his head. "How was your bath? Feel better? You smell good."

She responded quietly, "Yes, it was good. I do feel better."

He could tell that she had not moved from the doorway so he asked her, "Are you coming in here? Why are you standing in the doorway?"

"I need you to do something," she stated.

"Sure, whatever you need. What is it?" He still had not opened his eyes.

"Well, I need you to come in here with me." She still didn't say where she wanted him to come so he opened his eyes and turned to look at her.

"In where? The bathroom? The bedroom? The kitchen? What's wrong?"

"Nothing's wrong," she smirked. "Just come with me." She tugged on the belt of her silk robe. He could tell she was naked underneath. It finally dawned on him what she was asking.

He loved her shyness but it made him laugh. He sat up on the sofa and looked her up and down as he teased her. "Oh, okay Ms. Valerie. What did that water do to you? Is my baby horny? Your love jones has come down? You need a tune-up? You missing Jimbo?"

She rolled her eyes and asked, "Are you done with your questions? The answer is yes to all of those. So are you coming or not?" She was embarrassed but determined to get what she wanted. She wanted to feel him inside her and his weight on top of her. No special positions or games. Just straight carnal lovemaking and plenty of it. Who said they were too old for this?

He jumped up off the sofa and put his book away, telling her, "Happy to do whatever you need.

Glad you asked. You don't have to be shy. Say what you want. Feel free to come to me and just take my clothes off." He was still laughing when he got to her and wrapped his arms around her shoulder as they walked to the bedroom.

"Stop laughing at me." She elbowed him in his side. "I've never asked a man to make love to me before. This is all your fault anyway. You make me feel good. You make me want more."

As he undressed, he headed for the shower then leaned back into the bedroom to ask, "Any special requests Ms. Mason? Do you want handcuffs? A spanking? A special position? Give me some direction."

She got in bed shaking her head in disbelief of what he was asking. When he came back from the shower, he asked her more questions: "Whips? Chains? Your favorite sex toy?"

She answered him with a serious look saying, "No, keep it simple and make it good. Think you can do that Mr. Funnyman?" She couldn't help but laugh.

He slid in between the sheets, gave her the serious stare, and responded with a wink, "I'll give you my best. You can tell me after if it was good."

With that, they turned off the lights and found each other in the dark.

He knew exactly what she needed: long, slow, steady strokes, holding her tight and kissing her gently. No talking. She hardly moved at all, just taking him all in and feeling him love her from inside. It was intense, erotic, and very satisfying. They both moaned quietly then dozed off to sleep momentarily, still locked together. They woke up and headed for the bathroom, where he popped her on her butt with a towel and asked, 'Well? Was it good?"

"It was alright," she teased him with a big grin on her face while looking down, thanking Jimbo and giving him a special rub for his part in the evening festivities.

"Just Jimbo? No extra rub for me? I contributed a little bit." Jefferson asked, with a frown and a pout on his face before smiling.

She rubbed his back and said, "Oh yes, good job. Now hurry up, I'm sleepy."

They both had very content facial expressions as they headed to bed for the night. Before she dozed off, she whispered, "Thank you. I needed you." He rubbed her shoulder, saying, "I will always be here for you."

Chapter Twenty-Two

During the week, while Valerie and Jefferson worked and thought about wedding and honeymoon plans, their minds were never far from the issue of Valerie's divorce and Steven and Nikki. Steven finally called and asked to talk to them on Friday evening. They gave up date night to hear what he had to say.

By the time Steven and Jason got to Jefferson's house, Jason was sleepy so they put him in bed in one of the guest bedrooms. The adults all took a seat in the family room.

"First, let me tell you that I didn't know any of this was going to happen. It has knocked me off my feet and it's been a long, long week. But I am still very much interested in getting to know Nikki so I want to be as upfront with both of you as I can be." He looked exhausted but very sure of what he wanted to say.

He continued. "As you might expect, Ann is crushed. We talked all night on Sunday and a little bit every night this week. Just so you know the backstory, Ms. Val, Ann was best friends with my wife from kindergarten. They were more like sisters than many sisters I know. She was there in every way during Carla's pregnancy, and was the first person Carla called when she went into labor.

"Carla was a high risk pregnancy because she had blood clots, but she wanted to have a baby. My baby. She followed all the doctors' orders for bedrest and Ann was over several days a week to keep her company and keep her spirits up. I was glad Carla had someone to talk about baby stuff with while she waited because I had to work.

"Carla made it through delivery and we were all so happy. She was holding Jason when she started having chest pains and they found blockage where a clot had traveled to her heart. They couldn't dissolve it or stop it." He stopped talking and closed his eyes, remembering.

"As you can imagine, I went to pieces right there in the hospital when it happened. Mom and Uncle Jeff were there. Carla was my life and I could not get her to see that we would be okay without a child. Or that we could adopt. But she wanted my baby and ended up losing her life to have him."

"Mom took a couple weeks of family medical leave to take care of Jason and get all his clothes and feeding stuff together. Uncle Jeff helped Ann finish the nursery. Mom and Ann figured out the doctor visit schedule and the routine for eating and sleeping and the right formula. I was present, but just going through the motions until after the funeral. When Mom and Uncle Jeff started getting back to their lives, Ann offered to move in. She said it was her promise to Carla when she agreed to be his godmother to care for Jason if she couldn't and she intended to honor it. Thank God because it took me a while not to get mad when I looked at Jason, knowing he cost us both his mother.

"Ann taught me how to hold him and talk to him, clean him, feed him, everything. Including how to love him through the loss and bond with him. I owe her a huge debt of gratitude. I love her for it, but I love her like a sister. Like the sister she was to Carla and like the sister she became to me during my relationship and marriage to Carla.

"She tried to come on to me about a year or so after Carla died. I kept pushing her off saying I was flattered, but not interested in anyone like that yet. I was not ready. And besides, we were family. She waited another year or so then came to my room one night, telling me it was time to get back to the real world and she loved me and wanted us to try to have a relationship. She got in my bed and tried to kiss me but I felt nothing. Dead inside.

"We have been talking over the last few months about Jason being in school and she had time on her hands so she was going to go to school or get a part time job just to have something to do. She started hinting about us again and adding to the family and I finally said no to her in a firm, definite way. I think she was still hoping for one last shot until she saw me looking at Nikki. Then she knew for sure that I had never, and probably would never, look at her like that.

"She is looking for a place and we are talking to Jason about her moving out and it just being us guys. He and I are doing more together and less with her to ease her out of the house. I hope that by the time she actually moves we will all still be family, just in the way it would have been in the first place."

Valerie asked the key question. "What about Nikki?"

"So I need to take the next few weeks to get my new life together. Get Ann out of the house and me and Jason in our routine. By that time, I should be ready to see Nikki and we can talk. She might have made some decisions on her own. I really hope to get to know her though. I have not been this stirred up about any woman since Carla. She is not Carla, I get that, and we will have to establish our own relationship, but I would like to see where it could go.

"I want your blessing though. Maybe not tonight, but by the time I see Nikki again I would like to know if you would be okay with us dating."

Valerie gave her opinion. "I can appreciate your interest in Nikki. Aside from her being my daughter, I think she is a beautiful, loving human being. I don't know if she will be your first in this new awakening, or if she is the next Mrs. Steven Jackson. But I ask of you what I asked of Nikki, that you both tread very, very carefully, for everybody's sake, especially Jason's."

Jefferson finally spoke. "I'm glad you and Ann are working toward a good resolution to this whole situation. She is a very nice woman who deserves happiness. I am grateful to her for her sacrifices for Jason and you. I really like your plan for the next several weeks. Let us know if we can help with Jason as you figure out the new schedule."

Jefferson looked at Valerie to get her agreement and she nodded yes.

Steven looked at Valerie with a hopeful look and inquired, "Has she asked about me?"

Valerie responded honestly. "Yes. We also talk about your full life and the need to sort this out the right way, especially for Ann's sake. I think Nikki living in Chicago might help you guys keep some perspective."

They invited Steven to spend the night since it was late and he was obviously exhausted. He was happy to say yes. His uncle's house had always been a haven for him to rest and think and he needed that tonight. They both assured him that he was always welcome and they would always be there for him.

Chapter Twenty-Three

The next two weeks were peaceful and everyone got back to the routine of their lives. Valerie and Jefferson went to *Cafe 4212*, a jazz club, and a couple of restaurants during Restaurant Week. They were having such a good time together that they started getting excited again about getting married. They tried to figure out if they would be able to tell a difference in their relationship or their lifestyle after they were married. Both hoped it would stay the same because it was great. They had no idea how it would get even better but they were open to see how things progressed.

Jefferson decided to switch things up a bit with Valerie so he invited her to lunch on Thursday after she got off work at the flower shop. He was thinking that they would spend the rest of the afternoon together, maybe drive to Galveston so he could show her the building complex where he had part ownership. She liked the idea so he drove her to work then picked her up after.

They went to *Pappadeaux Seafood Kitchen* for lunch before they got on the road. He had the seafood gumbo and she had blackened catfish and rice. Valerie ordered crème brulee for dessert, and was just putting a spoonful in Jefferson's mouth to taste when she heard the voice she had been avoiding. It sounded very close so he had to be standing right next to the booth they were sitting in.

"See David, this is why we needed to meet today. She's not answering my calls, but someone else is obviously getting through." David was Vincent's attorney and they were meeting to discuss how to get Valerie to respond to Vincent's calls and what the courts could possibly do to help. He was getting desperate with only one court date left.

Jefferson looked up to see who was speaking and knew immediately that it had to be Vincent. He looked at Valerie who whispered, "Looks like today is the day for the games to begin. Are you ready?" He whispered back, "Ready if you are." She whispered to him, "I love you," and he whispered back, "Good to know," while nodding.

Valerie put the spoon down and turned around to look up and down at Vincent and David. She had a blank expression and waited for one of them to speak.

David said hello with an apologetic look on his face. He always thought Vincent was stupid for cheating on her and had told that to his friend. He still represented him, however, and ultimately he helped Valerie get a good settlement.

David had reasoned with Vincent that if he wanted a chance to get his wife back, he had to show her his generous, caring side, as well as his appreciation of their life together by making sure she continued to have a good life that he provided. The other argument he used was the impact a bad financial settlement for Valerie on top of cheating could have on his relationship with his daughter. If Nikki found out that her dad would not give her mother what she deserved, Vincent knew that he would never be able to repair their relationship.

Now David was trying to get Vincent to let go and sign the papers but Vincent refused. He really wanted his wife back and thought she should, and eventually would, forgive him. David was not interested in a confrontation so he tried to steer Vincent to their table. He was not successful.

Vincent spoke to Jefferson first. "You do know that she is still married. To me."

Jefferson nodded his head in affirmation, giving him the 'Ware stare.' "I do know. And yet she's here with me."

Jefferson's response was so confident, bordering on cocky, that it pissed Vincent off and he turned to Valerie. "You have missed the calls we are supposed to have each week and the last counseling sessions. We need to talk. Are you trying to drag this out for months? "

"No," Valerie responded. "I'm actually hoping that you will get the message that I am not coming back to you and sign the papers. We could be done today."

"Well I'm not giving up on us. At least make some time to hear me out. You might like what I have to say." Vincent was like a dog with a bone. He was not giving up without a fight, especially now that he had seen her with another man. They looked a little too cozy for his liking so he knew he had to move fast.

David was standing behind Vincent giving Valerie a sympathetic look, hoping that she would say yes to Vincent so they could go to their table and have lunch. Jefferson had leaned back in the booth and put his arm behind Valerie, watching the scene play out.

Valerie finally said, "Call me tomorrow afternoon at one and I will answer. Now have a good lunch." She was dismissive in both her words and tone, as she turned back around to Jefferson. Vincent sat at a table with David making sure he faced the booth where Valerie was sitting so he could look at her as long as possible, and she could see him and maybe remember some of their good times when they had gone out together.

Jefferson winked at her and said, "Look at you talking all feisty and strong. That's a sexy look on you V. We might have to get a room in Galveston and work off some of the tension you're carrying in that fine body."

"Sounds good to me," Valerie responded, ready to go but not wanting to rush out as if Vincent had spoiled their lunch. They had the rest of the Crème Brulee wrapped to go and Jefferson paid the bill.

The ride to Galveston was quiet at first, as they both thought about what had happened at the restaurant and what was to come with Vincent Mason. Then Valerie turned to Jefferson and said, "I missed having the rest of my dessert. Except I think I want to share it with Jimbo this time. Do you think he would mind if I lick the Crème Brulee off him? Do you think he would mind getting a little sticky so I could make you scream for a change?"

Jefferson looked over at her in shock, trying not to run off the road. He told her, "I might not mind if the divorce took another few months to be finalized if the encounters with your ex make you talk like that." They both started laughing and she said, "Round One to Team Ware." Jefferson knew there would likely be more rounds so he was happy for the moment but did not get too excited.

Chapter Twenty-Four

Vincent's tone on the call the next day at one was very different from his attitude at *Pappadeaux*'s. Today he was kind and conciliatory, trying to seduce Valerie with memories of good times together and their greatest accomplishment, their daughter Nikki. He also apologized for what he had done and the way things turned out.

"I made a mistake Val. A few of them. I knew you were unhappy for a long time but I was too busy making money to figure out what the problems really were and give you what you asked of me. Or to admit that maybe we had grown apart. I wasn't exciting enough for you. I know. I knew a long time ago that you were more woman than I had ever had but I was glad you said yes and ignored the warning signs that things weren't right. We could have fixed some of that. Trina was a huge mistake. She wanted the promotion -- not me. I gave her what she wanted, moved her to our Atlanta office, and have been alone ever since. I'm sorry and I miss you." Valerie did not respond, just listened to gauge his sincerity.

He continued. "I've been going to our sessions with the therapist without you to help me understand why I dared cheat on such a fabulous woman. I'm also reading and listening to some of these relationship coaches on podcasts and YouTube the therapist recommended to learn how to loosen up and try different ways to please you. I just hope it's not too late and you will at least give us a shot. I'm even about ready to retire so we could do some of the things we talked about, traveling the states and revisiting some of the countries we visited when we were dating." He paused so that she could respond.

Valerie's tone was kind as well. "Thank you for the apology. I don't know what you are learning in therapy, but I am definitely interested in knowing why you cheated. And why you didn't even talk to me first before you decided to risk our marriage." Then all of the feelings came flooding back and the pitch of her voice rose in agitation. "Actually I had not felt good about you or us for a long time. When I learned what was occupying your mind and your time, that just seemed to wipe away all thirty years of me loving you and being a good wife and mother to your child. That's why I'm really not interested in us getting back together."

You could hear the air escape Vincent's mouth. He had been holding his breath, praying for a sign that she would be open to communicating on a regular basis. It was going to be an uphill battle.

He tried another approach. "I see you are dating now. Will you at least go on a date with me? Just one? Dinner. Wherever you want to go. At least let us talk like this some more but face to face."

Valerie hesitated. She wondered what Jefferson would think of that and decided to ask him later that day when they talked about the call. To Vincent she said, "I'll think about it. Give me a week and we can talk again. I need to go now. Let's talk again next week, same time." She hung up and sat quietly in the den to think about what Vincent had said. That's where she was when Jefferson came home. It was Friday and he had finished his day earlier than usual, in part because he was anxious to get home and talk to Valerie, then they would decide whether to go on a date that night.

Jefferson called to her as soon as he walked in the house. Her car was in the garage so he knew she was at home. She responded softly from the den so he headed there and paused in the doorway. She looked up at him and smiled a slow, pensive smile. He walked over and sat on the sofa, pulling her into his arms and massaging her head. It always relaxed her and excited him to be in the thickness of her hair.

"How are you?" He asked first.

"I'm good actually. How are you? How was your day?" She was pleasant, but not giving any signs to him of how the call went.

"Good. Are you going to make it better and tell me you got him to agree to sign the papers?" He was hopeful but figured it was not going to be that easy.

"No such luck," Valerie reported. "But I got a sincere apology for ruining our marriage, and news that he is using the therapy sessions to be a better man."

Jefferson nodded and exhaled. "What else?" There was always more with Valerie.

"He asked me out on a date. My terms of when and where. What do you think?"

"I think you should tell me what you want. What would you like to get from the date? What else do you want to hear from him?" They were pointed questions, the very ones that Valerie had been thinking about since the call.

"Actually, I don't want a date. Just a meeting to keep talking about our issues, just to clear the air. I guess I need more vindication. He was so mean and ugly to me for a long while when he was lying and cheating; I just want to get something that makes me feel good so I can be civil to him going forward, not just when there is an emergency with Nikki."

Jefferson didn't respond right away but kept massaging her head slowly. His suggestion surprised Valerie. "Why don't you ask for a meeting in the attorney's office? A conference room with just you and him. Then if he finally agrees, you can get the papers signed before you leave. If he doesn't sign, at least it will have been in neutral territory and you would not be uncomfortable."

Valerie liked the idea and said she would propose it to Vincent on their next call. In the meantime, she was happy to be with Jefferson and they decided to skip their weekly Salsa class and go out for tacos and ice cream and to ride around so Jefferson could show her where all of his houses were in Third Ward before it got dark.

One thing she learned on their next call was that Vincent was not going away quietly. He knew she would not pick up the phone until Friday so he left loving voicemail messages for her. He sent flowers on Monday to her building, hoping it would keep him on her mind during the week. Since she was not there, the staff on duty called her. She asked them to put the flowers on display in the lobby and put the card under her door.

Vincent bought her gifts—candles of her favorite scent that she liked to burn when taking a bath; a picture frame with a picture in it of him, her and Nikki when Nikki was about ten years old; the newest books by her favorite female authors; and pearl earrings from Tiffany's. Had to give him credit, Valerie thought, he was trying. It was too little too late, however, and the more time she spent with Jefferson, the more sure she was of her decision to marry him.

Vincent would attempt to drop off his gifts to her building, hoping that he would get a chance to personally deliver them to her apartment. She was never home. The doormen knew she was with Jefferson but they never told Vincent. After the third visit and Valerie was not home, Vincent got suspicious and he left a message for Valerie to explain where she was and when she would be home so he could bring the gifts he had for her. Valerie never answered that question when she talked to him on Friday.

He refused an office meeting and insisted they have dinner. "It's the least you can do since you are dating someone else. I want equal opportunity to spend time with you." She was hoping that if she gave in to the date, he would finally see that no matter what he did, she did not want him back. She decided to talk to Jefferson again about one dinner date with Vincent to try to get the papers signed.

Chapter Twenty-Five

The question of the date caused a lot of tension between Valerie and Jefferson. "I thought we had settled that Valerie? I don't trust Vincent and what he might do to you if you go out with him. He is getting angry and desperate. Not a good combination. Why is this so important for you to do? Do you want to go on a date with him?"

"No, I don't want to. I want him to sign the papers and if one date will do it then I want to give him a couple of hours one evening and get it over with."

Jefferson fired back, "What makes you think he will sign after the date? I think it's a ploy for him to get you relaxed and to reconsider your marriage. I don't like it. I don't want you out with him, or his hands on you, or him using thirty years of knowing you in marriage to get you to see him as a great man and husband. Don't do it. Please." His level of anxiety was on twenty and it seemed to him that she did not grasp the importance of what this meant to him.

Then Valerie got testy with Jefferson. "So what you are really saying is that you don't trust me, trust that I don't want him and can handle a date with him? It's just one time Jefferson. Or are you thinking of Alicia and what she did to you? Well I am not Alicia. I love you and I need you to trust me and trust that I know Vincent and believe this will work. Can you do that?"

Jefferson made a final plea. "What I am saying is I thought we were Team Ware, fighting him together. I don't like you being on a date with him and don't want you to go. I trust *you* but not him. Everything in me is screaming no. I just wish you would trust *me*. I know how men are and this is not feeling right at all."

He walked away from her saying he would be back, going to visit his best friend from the Air Force, Zeke. He was hoping they would play a little basketball in Zeke's yard and relieve some of the stress the discussion had caused. He believed that she was probably going out with Vincent and he started to brace himself for what would happen. He knew in his soul it would not be good but he decided to wait and see what transpired. He loved Valerie and wanted her more than anything, but it was important that she want him too. She said she did, but her insistence on going on this date made him wonder. Was it her ego making her believe she could handle Vincent – the Vincent who cheated on her?

Valerie went into the den to wrestle with her dilemma. On the one hand, she was surprised at Jefferson's anxiety about her having a couple of hours with Vincent. It was okay in a counselors or lawyers office but not in a public restaurant? Was he really that jealous and fearful that she would go back with Vincent?

She called Lillian to get another perspective, explaining Vincent's recent behavior and request for a date, Jefferson's pleas for her not to go out on the date, and her rationale for going to try to use the date to speed up the divorce. Lillian was very quiet, listening until Valerie asked for her thoughts.

Lillian took a deep breath and said, "You might not want to hear this, but I love you and will always tell you the truth about what I feel. I agree with Jefferson. Don't go. Over the last three years or so Vincent cheated on you, lied to you, embarrassed you, and moved on with his life. He never cared about your marriage or your feelings during all of that time. Now he's acting like he can't live without you. You are better than being treated like that. You have a man who excites you, loves you, and wants to marry you. Why jeopardize that for one date with a snake? Especially one who will probably not sign the divorce papers and will come up with another excuse to be with you. Don't go. Let Vincent know that you have moved on and let Jefferson know that he's more important to you than Vincent ever will be again. The judge will grant you a divorce soon enough. Just wait a little longer."

Valerie couldn't think of any counterpoints to what Lillian said and expressed her appreciation for Lillian's honesty and friendship. After hanging up with her, Valerie realized that she was still looking for vindication and closure from Vincent. She figured out that she needed to let go of vindication because there was no excuse for him cheating, and let the divorce be the closure. She also realized that if it were

Jefferson asking for a date with Alicia or another soon to be ex, she would not like it either.

Her decision was made. There would be no date with Vincent. Now Valerie had to get Vincent to back off and still sign the papers. Or just wait for the judge to grant the divorce.

When Jefferson came home, Valerie had dinner waiting and an "I'm sorry, you are right, I'm not going" speech ready. Jefferson walked in from the garage, looked at the stove but not at Valerie and said, "Thanks for dinner, but I'm not hungry." He took a shower and went straight to bed. It wasn't even eight o'clock so Valerie knew she had hurt his feelings deeply.

She cleaned up the kitchen, changed into her nightclothes, and crawled in bed with him but he wasn't in his usual position on his back waiting for her. He was facing the wall. She tried to pull his arm to get him to roll onto his back but he pulled away from her. She felt the rejection immediately so she molded her body to his back and butt with her leg on top of his and told him in his ear that he was right about her not going out with Vincent and she was sorry for upsetting him and keeping them from a nice evening together. They laid like that for about an hour, neither sleeping. Finally, he rolled over so she could lay on him but he didn't put his arm around her or say a word. They both fell asleep.

Chapter Twenty-Six

A week later, on Saturday night, as they settled into bed, Valerie's cell phone rang. It was after midnight so they both sensed there was trouble on the other end of the line. Memorial Hermann Hospital was calling for Mrs. Valerie Mason, the wife of Vincent Mason, and designated decision-maker according to his medical directive.

"I'm not his wife anymore. We have not been together for over two years. Surely he has given you another directive with someone else designated. His brother or sister? His daughter, Veronica?" She was talking to the doctor in charge of his case, Dr. Grant, and she insisted that Valerie Mason was the only name she had. Vincent had been in a terrible accident and they needed to notify the family. He was unconscious and would be having surgery to repair his broken leg and arm. Valerie took her name and number and promised to pass the information on to Vincent's family.

When she hung up, Jefferson was sitting up with the light on waiting to hear what was going on.

"Vincent's been in an accident, and since he never changed his Medical Directive, I was the one they called. He's at Memorial Hermann Hospital in the Woodlands. He's not conscious and needs surgery. I'm going to call Nikki and his brother and sister so they can all start preparing to head to Houston."

She went in the den to make the calls so Jefferson could go back to sleep. She called his brother first since he was coming from California, then his sister who would drive from Dallas, then Nikki who begged Valerie to go to the hospital to see about him until she could get there in the morning from Chicago. Valerie protested, giving her the doctor's name and number so she could get updates directly. That was not enough for Nikki who pressed her mom to go actually see him and let her know what was going on.

"I know you guys have issues and you have no interest in his life, but he's my dad and he's unconscious! He's all alone and I would hate for him to be in the hospital by himself and, heaven forbid, something else happens to him. I just want him to know that one of us is with him. Please mom. Just until I get there."

Valerie gave in to her and went back to the bedroom to get dressed. When she told Jefferson what Nikki asked of her, Jefferson started getting dressed too. Valerie noticed and commented, "You don't have to go. Only one of us needs to have this headache tonight. Tag, I'm it." She said it with a heavy sigh.

He looked at her as if she had grown a third eye. "I'm not going to let you go out of this house at this time of night and drive over thirty miles to the Woodlands alone. You are already tired and this is a stressful situation. I can drive while you relax until we get there. It is going to be a long night. Plus I want to make sure you are taken care of, with water and food, while you take care of whatever you need to take care of with your ex, for Nikki's sake."

She hesitated and slowly finished getting dressed. He could tell she was thinking about something.

"What is it? You don't want me to go?" He was surprised and getting annoyed.

"It's not that. I just don't know what I'll find when I get there and I was just trying to spare you a long, boring night sitting around in a hospital."

"I've been in hospitals before Valerie. I know what sitting around waiting is like. I can handle it." He stopped dressing to ask her, "What's the real deal V? You don't want me to see your other family? Or you don't want them to see me?" He waited for her to answer. When she took too long, he walked out of the room saying, "Oh. Okay. Well then be safe," and went to the den.

She went running after him. "No Jefferson, that's not it. Please. I want you to come with me. You will meet them eventually anyway. I have nothing to hide. It just feels strange."

"Don't lie to me Valerie. I told you before, I don't want to be anywhere you don't want me. You've got a lot on you already. I don't want to add to it. You go. I'll see you whenever you get back." He turned the television on to shift his focus and try to diffuse his attitude.

She took the remote out of his hands, turned the television off, and turned his face to hers. "I want you to go with me. I need you, your strength, your presence. It would be nice to have you by my side. Please. I'm sorry if I didn't say that properly up front. I just want to do this for Nikki so she doesn't get any more upset. Plus I can see how bad Vincent really is and prepare Nikki when she gets here."

Jefferson paused before speaking, looking at her closely. "That was a good save," he told her with a half-smile. "Put it on Nikki and you know I can't say no." He pushed her to get up so they could go. They took a moment to hug first. She was drawing strength, and he was reminding her that he loved her.

In the car, Valerie called Dr. Grant to let her know that she was on the way to the hospital, and what time she expected to arrive. Valerie was on edge, thinking that this could prolong the divorce, and she was deeply troubled about that.

Chapter Twenty-Seven

When Valerie and Jefferson walked in to the emergency room, two of Vincent's friends were waiting and met her and Jefferson just inside the door. They had seen her walking up to the door from the emergency parking lot and wanted to make sure she saw them in the crowded waiting area. "What's going on Stan? Hey Richard." She was not surprised his best friends from college were there. "Were you with him tonight?"

They both nodded while looking at Jefferson, wondering who he was but didn't ask. "It looks bad Val," Stan responded. "We were coming back from a motorcycle riding event and it started raining so the pavement was slick. All of a sudden, a drunk driver swerved in front of our line and hit Vincent hard on the rear tire of his bike. He went flying right into the highway divider about 200 yards away. We thought he was dead because the impact was so hard, you could hear bones cracking."

"Bike? You mean motorcycle?" She was stunned. Mr. Conservative Vincent on a motorcycle? Was this some sort of post mid-life crisis? He had never mentioned a motorcycle on their calls.

They shook their heads yes. "We got them last year. Usually we all ride together and nothing happens." They were still looking at Jefferson so Valerie introduced them.

"This is Jefferson, my soon to be husband." To Jefferson she shared, "These are Vincent's best friends from college and now they are apparently sharing a motorcycle life." She rolled her eyes. The men nodded at each other.

"We have to wait down here since we are not family so anything you can tell us would be great."

"Of course. Let me see what's going on and I'll come back down." Valerie liked them and knew they were close with Vincent.

Valerie and Jefferson stopped at the desk then headed to the ICU floor where they had assigned Vincent a room. The female doctor, Dr. Grant, was waiting for them when they got off the elevator.

"Your husband was on a motorcycle, got hit by a drunk driver, and was reportedly thrown off his bike then propelled head first into a concrete highway divider. He is unconscious, we believe from head trauma as a result of the contact with the divider. We are assessing the severity to determine our course of action.

"His left arm and leg are broken, taking a big hit against the concrete when he was thrown off the bike. He had on gloves but his arms are scraped pretty bad, maybe from trying to stop. We call it road rash and it usually happens when bike riders don't have on leather jackets or similar type of covering to protect the skin. Not a surprise since it's a typical hot Houston summer. We are running an MRI and CT scan to see what internal damage has been done to his brain, bones, and wrists, then we need to reset his leg and do surgery on his arm. What is his blood type? Do you know what medications he is currently taking?"

The doctor was talking to Valerie but looking at Jefferson. She looked puzzled, as if she was trying to place him.

"For the record, one more time, he is my ex, not my husband. I'm just here until our daughter arrives so do what you need to do for him. His blood type is O, and he used to keep a list of medications and supplements he takes in his wallet. As I recall he wasn't taking much medicine—something for high cholesterol and eye drops for dry eye. I haven't kept up with his health in over three years so check his wallet." Valerie noticed the doctor looking at Jefferson so she looked at him to see if he was looking at her too. He was looking at Valerie.

Dr. Grant led them to the family waiting area, promising that she would come back to give them updates as soon as possible whenever Vincent was done with all of the tests, and again when he was out of surgery.

Valerie and Jefferson sat in a two-person settee to wait. He stretched his long legs out in front of him and leaned back with his head against the wall and eyes closed. He was not asleep, just wanted to relax while they waited. Valerie called Nikki to let her know that she and Jefferson were at the hospital but had not seen Vincent yet, and updated her on the doctor's report. She leaned back too, leaning on Jefferson's shoulder while they waited.

Dr. Grant came back to announce that the tests confirmed their suspicions. "Mr. Mason sustained a moderate traumatic brain injury which is why he lost consciousness. He had on a helmet, which helped buffer some of the impact, but the force was so strong when he hit the concrete divider that his head was still shaken, and hard. His brain is slightly swollen. He could be out for a while, and I can't tell you when he might wake up. He has a broken tibia and fibula and broken ankle to his left leg, his left wrist and arm are broken too and need to be reset, and three cracked ribs. We are waiting for a surgical room to open up and expect he will be in surgery for a couple of hours as we make the repairs." The wait would continue.

Valerie went downstairs to give Stan and Richard the update and encouraged them to go home. She promised to call them after surgery. They were clearly shaken by what had happened and did not want to leave but agreed that they would rest up and be ready to help with Vincent's recovery.

When Valerie got back to the family waiting area, the doctor was sitting in Val's seat on the settee talking very animatedly with Jefferson. Valerie stood in the doorway and watched. Jefferson was still leaning back with his arms crossed, but he was looking at the doctor, smiling then laughing. They clearly knew each other.

When she walked up to them, Jefferson sat up and reached out for her to come to him. The doctor turned to look Valerie up and down, like she was seeing her for the first time.

Valerie sat in Jefferson's lap and he re-introduced them while he rubbed her arms. "Valerie, this is Debra Grant. Dr. Grant. She went to med school with my ex, Alicia. What a small world. Deb, this is Valerie, *my* soon to be wife, Vincent Mason's ex."

Dr. Grant gave Valerie a polite smile and said, "Congratulations. You've got a good one."

"I know," Valerie gushed and smiled at Jefferson. "So you were friends with Alicia and Jeff?"

"Actually more friends with Jeff after Alicia divorced him. He's the one that got away." Her inflection was clear. They had slept together and she had liked him.

They paged the doctor so she got up to leave. She promised to come back so they could spend more time catching up.

Valerie sat down next to Jefferson. "So you slept with her?"

Jefferson answered honestly. "Yes. But we didn't date. It was more of a convenience thing until I figured out what I was going to do with myself after the divorce. That's probably why I didn't recognize her right away. I try not to think about or remember too much about that time. "

"You do realize she liked you and wanted more?"

"How did you get all that from the last five minutes?" He was surprised to hear her say that. He thought so at the time, years ago, but had made it clear to Deb that he was not interested. For him, anyone in the medical field was off limits after what Alicia had done to him.

"Because of the way she was leaning in to you and touching you and smiling at you. She wants more now. She must not be married?" It was a statement but she asked in a question.

"No. She said she just got here from Cleveland Clinic and was settling in to the area."

"Okay Mr. Ware. You are on notice. She is going to come back to ask to spend some time with you, help her get settled. So don't act crazy and make me have to visit you out here in one of these beds after I cut you for cheating on me."

He laughed and hugged her, nuzzling his face in her neck saying, "No worries. I'm happy with you. I don't want or need anyone else." Valerie sat in her seat next to Jefferson and they both fell asleep.

As soon as the cafeteria opened, Jefferson went down for coffee and breakfast for them. While there, he called Jeannette to cancel Game Day, explaining where he was and what had happened. "Valerie's ex, Vincent, has been in an accident and is in the hospital. We are here to see what's going on until Nikki gets in from Chicago. Let Steven know too and I'll talk to you guys tomorrow." Jefferson didn't want to talk to Steven because he knew Steven would probably ask whether he could see Nikki and Jefferson didn't think it was time for that yet. They needed to find out what was going on with Ann before they would consider connecting Steven and Nikki to get to know each other.

Just as they finished eating breakfast, a woman came down the hallway looking for the family room.

She spotted Valerie and ran towards her. Valerie stood up. "Hey lady." They greeted each other with a hug. Valerie introduced Viveca, Vincent's sister, who looked Jefferson up and down and commented that she understood why Val was looking so good. "You go girl. I am not mad at you at all!" Jefferson smiled, flattered.

Valerie filled her in on Vincent's status and they all stood together when Dr. Grant came back after surgery. "His broken leg and arm and ribs will heal, but over time. Six to eight weeks, maybe a little longer given his age. And he will definitely need rehab for occupational and physical therapy. He will stay in the hospital until he wakes up and gets evaluated again then go to a rehab facility or home. You all need to decide who will manage his care. He will need it 24/7 until the casts are off, less as he learns to take care of himself again."

Valerie and Viveca were allowed to see Vincent briefly in ICU but only for about ten minutes. They were not surprised that he was all bandaged up, but his face was very pale. He looked dead, not just sleeping. Viveca started crying. Valerie was concerned about how Nikki would react so she had to be sure to be there when she saw Vincent for the first time.

Valerie was about to reach out to Nikki again but saw two text messages. Victor, the brother, would arrive at noon and so would Nikki, both coming in at Hobby Airport. Jefferson offered to pick them up while Valerie stayed at the hospital. Valerie decided that by then she would want a break so they would both go to the airport. Viveca could stay with Vincent.

    The doctor came back at the end of her shift to give Jefferson her card and asked if they could catch up later. Valerie watched Jefferson drop the card in her purse. Debra Grant watched too and got the message that there would be no catching up without Valerie. When Dr. Grant walked away, Valerie gave Jefferson a big hug and they looked at each other with a smile.

Chapter Twenty-Eight

Nikki and Checkers arrived first, and Nikki's eyes were red from fatigue. She hugged Jefferson then held her mom so tight Valerie could hardly breathe. She wanted a full report on her dad's condition. Valerie asked her to wait for her Uncle Vic so she could just say it once.

They both spotted Victor at the same time and Nikki went running, calling out for him. He gave her a big hug and kiss on her forehead and followed her to the car. He hugged Valerie for way too long, kissed her on both cheeks and gave her a long, loving look that was crystal clear. Jefferson knew immediately that he was in love with Valerie and had been for a long time. The forlorn look underneath the smile said Victor thought Valerie married the wrong brother.

When she introduced Jefferson as her fiancé, a look passed between him and Victor that said Jefferson knew Victor's feelings for Valerie and Victor knew that Jefferson could see his heart was breaking again. There was a silent, man-to-man agreement never to talk about it. Valerie saw the look but acted like she was busy talking to Nikki. She would definitely ask Jefferson about it later.

Valerie explained Vincent's condition as they headed to the hospital and she tried to prepare them for how he looked in his face and with all the bandages and casts on his arm and leg. "It's going to be a long road to recovery, at least six to eight weeks, so you all are going to have to make some decisions, including where he will recover and who will be on his Medical Directive. You have to take my name off."

When Nikki saw Vincent, the usually strong, take charge woman felt weak. It was the first time she had ever seen her dad in a hospital or looking less than strong and powerful. Until he cheated, he was her hero. Now he looked helpless.

He was very pale and lifeless with a PICC line for getting meds. He did not respond to her voice calling his name or saying that she loved him. The thought that she could lose her dad was frightening. She kept saying to Valerie that he had to wake up, he couldn't die. She held on to Valerie until the doctor in charge during the day shift assured them that Vincent was extremely lucky.

"I have seen much worse. In my professional opinion, Vincent will recover, it will just take a while. I did not see any serious brain damage on the scans. There is swelling for sure, probably from the hard bang on the concrete when he flew off the bike. It will take a minute for his brain to settle back down. Thankfully, there was no bleeding or cracked skull, which we attribute to him wearing a helmet and the way he probably tried to stop or protect himself with his left side. He should wake up at some point soon, but for sure he will need to learn to walk on crutches, and it will be weeks of occupational or physical therapy to get him able to take care of himself."

The ICU allowed only one person to visit per hour and only for ten to fifteen minutes at a time. They let Viveca and Valerie go in together when they were getting Vincent settled in from surgery. Valerie went in with Nikki during Nikki's first visit to Vincent's room. Nikki was clearly distraught and the staff appreciated her mother being there to comfort her. Going forward, visiting would be limited to one person at a time.

Viveca and Victor asked to stay the rest of the day and night. Valerie and Jefferson could take Nikki and Checker's to Vincent's house to get settled and Nikki could see what shape the house and cars were in. Viveca had driven from Dallas so she would drive herself and Victor to Vincent's house. Victor and Nikki would each use one of Vincent's two cars while they were in town.

The Mason's also decided that it made no sense for all of them to be at the hospital at the same time since they had to adhere to the schedule for visiting Vincent in his room. They decided to take shifts. Nikki got the day shift starting the next day, Monday. Viveca would come in the afternoon, and Victor in the evening, staying as late as the hospital would allow. They were hoping one of them would be on site at the hospital, if not in the room with Vincent, when he woke up.

Valerie and Jefferson took Nikki and Checkers to Vincent's house. They all went in to make sure everything was okay since Vincent had been away for a few days on his motorcycle trip. Valerie and Nikki checked whether the bedrooms were ready for guests, what laundry needed to be done, and what groceries were needed from the store. Jefferson made sure the cars started and had gas.

Jefferson took a moment to notice how his "competition" lived and determined that he was definitely an upper middle class guy. He had a nice two level home with quality furnishings. Everything was in neutral, beige colors. Well-coordinated, but boring. Vanilla. Nothing like the color he saw in Valerie's place or that he had in his own home. If this was representative of the man, no wonder Valerie was looking for excitement. That thought brought a smile to his face.

He watched Valerie look around her ex's house to see if she was interested in or even curious about how he was living or what woman's touch or belongings she would find. Jefferson looked relieved to see that Valerie had no reaction whatsoever to being in Vincent's space. She focused her attention on what Nikki needed to do to get settled. In just over an hour, Jefferson and Valerie left.

On Monday, Nikki asked her mom to come to the hospital on her days off from the flower shop and sit with her to keep her company. Nikki had called her boss for emergency vacation time so she was off work for two weeks and did not have any projects to do, but she promised to check email and take urgent calls on her cell. The rest of the time, she would be by herself and she wanted company when she was not in her dad's ICU room. The plan was that Valerie would come to the hospital only until Vincent woke up and was moved to a private room.

Valerie spoke with Jefferson about it that evening after work, assuring him that she would be there for Nikki, not to be with Vincent. He said he was fine with it since it would give the mother and daughter time together that they didn't usually have since they lived in separate cities. He even promised to come out one day and sit with them too so he and Nikki could have some time together as well. The agreement was that Valerie would work on Monday and Thursday and come home for the evening, then go to the hospital to sit with Nikki on Tuesday, Wednesday, and Friday, leaving her weekends for him.

The next day, Tuesday, Valerie went to the hospital right at the end of morning rush hour, arriving at about ten. She saw her roles as company keeper and mother, making sure Nikki ate and had plenty of water and even took a nap during the day to offset some of the stress she was going through.

Viveca arrived at three pm, with a report on Checkers, and what she had cooked so Nikki would have food when she got home. But neither Nikki nor Valerie left at that time, realizing that they would get caught in Houston's notoriously heavy evening rush hour traffic so they stayed until it was about over.

Victor came to the hospital before they could leave so they stayed a little longer to provide medical updates and just have a few minutes together. The Mason's were a close-knit family but since they were each living in different cities it was rare that they all got together. They were enjoying seeing each other, even under the circumstances of Vincent being incapacitated for now. His prognosis was good so they could just focus on him waking up, then decide how to handle his long-term care.

Chapter Twenty-Nine

On Monday evening, Valerie started getting a lot of phone calls from other Mason family members and many friends who had heard from Stan and Richard about Vincent's accident and Valerie being at the hospital. They wanted to talk with her about his condition, and whether she and Vincent were getting back together. She had cut off ties with most family and friends during the separation and divorce proceedings, but now people were happy to reconnect with her.

Jefferson didn't hear her responses on all of her calls, but for those he did, he heard her say they definitely were not getting back together. What he never heard her say, however, was that she was not going back to Vincent because she was getting married to someone else. He made a mental note of her lack of full disclosure, deciding to just be watchful and stay positive.

She apologized to Jefferson for the many phone calls that were disturbing their evening. Even Victor called her with an update and to say goodnight. She told the rest of the people she would call them back the next day from the hospital. There were so many that even though she stopped answering and let them go to voicemail, the mood was broken for her and Jefferson to have a good night together.

On Tuesday evening, Valerie called Jefferson to say she would be late because of traffic but by then he was already on edge. His question on why she hadn't left earlier so she could avoid rush hour was met with silence. Jefferson finally commented quietly, "I just don't want you to forget that you are on Team Ware now so the Mason's don't need you all day every day." Her response was curt. "I know that, and I know when to come home." On that note, they both hung up without saying good-bye.

It was quiet in the house when she arrived. Jefferson was in the kitchen at the table, scrolling through his phone so she walked over and gave him a half-hearted swipe on his lips. Jefferson pulled her close and held her for a moment, looking in her face. She would not look at him and immediately pulled away, going directly to the bedroom to shower and change into her nightclothes. He knew he had hit a hot button for her, but she had also hit one for him. It felt to him like a battle of wills and he wondered where this was leading. When he was ready for bed, he noticed that she was facing away from where he would be when he got in bed. He laid down in bed for a few minutes, but when she didn't roll over to him, he got up and slept on the couch in the den.

The next morning he was up, dressed, and in the kitchen early as usual but she stayed in bed later than usual. Since she had not come into the kitchen for their morning time together, he knew it was her way of saying she did not want to interact with him. He left without saying goodbye. When she knew he was gone, she got dressed and went back to the hospital.

On Wednesday afternoon when Nikki went in to say she was leaving for the day, Vincent was blinking his eyes and moaning, slowly regaining consciousness. His eyes opened completely for the first time and she cried, telling him how happy she was to see his eyes open and that it was the first sign that he was really recovering. She called for the nurse who welcomed him back while taking his vitals.

He could not talk initially because his throat was really dry and they didn't want him to have too much ice or water too quickly, but he could blink his eyes, once for yes, two for no, and grunt to get the attention of whoever was in the room.

Nikki told him she had a surprise for him and left the room, sending Valerie in to see that he was awake. Tears stood in his eyes when he saw her. He was excited to see that she had come to the hospital to see about him in his time of need, hoping that it meant she still had feelings for him. Then he noticed that Valerie didn't seem particularly excited to see him awake. He was disappointed. He couldn't even see sympathy in her eyes or her voice as she shared with him in a very dry, matter-of-fact tone that Stan and Richard were waiting for an update so she would call them, and she identified several of the family members who had called and sent their love. When she asked if he understood, he blinked once, meaning yes. She asked if there was anyone else he wanted her to call. He blinked twice for no.

He tried to talk to her but his voice was too weak. He knew then that from their phone calls and her expression there in the hospital, she really wasn't interested in him anymore and he would have to seriously consider letting her go. He became sad, bordering on depressed.

Nikki and Valerie waited in the family room while Viveca, then Victor, went in to see him. They were all excited and grateful that he was awake. Valerie reminded them of the need to put someone else on the medical directive and decide on his long-term care. They agreed to get Vincent's input before making any change.

Dr. Grant was on duty. She examined Vincent and talked to the family about next steps: there would be more tests scheduled for the next day to see how Vincent's brain was doing, then he would go to a regular room for the rest of the day to be sure he didn't lose consciousness again. He would probably be released by dinnertime. The hospital would need their decision in 24 hours on whether Vincent was going to rehab or home.

Vincent of course wanted to go home instead of to a rehab facility so he could be with his family. Victor and Viveca decided to leave on Sunday since Vincent was awake and starting to recover. They would help Nikki get him settled at the house. Then Nikki would have to decide how many weeks of FMLA she would take and how they could schedule trading off taking care of Vincent until he could take care of himself. Stan and Richard volunteered to take turns coming over to help with Vincent's care. Vincent pressed Valerie to take a turn in the schedule to take care of him but her answer was a very firm, very definite no.

They decided to get a hospital bed for Vincent to sleep in on his first floor, in the media room, hired a home health aide to get him bathed and ready for the day, and scheduled in-home occupational and physical therapy. Viveca was going home on Sunday so she could get back to work as a police officer and come to Houston every week-end to give Nikki a break. Victor had to get back to his tech security business, but he would come back every two weeks and stay for a week until his brother was mobile.

Valerie went home late again, this time happy to tell Jefferson the good news about Vincent waking up and her hopes for getting him to sign the divorce papers. Until she remembered that they weren't speaking. He was eating dinner when she walked in so she nodded then went to the bedroom to change clothes while waiting for him to finish in the kitchen.

He was in the den when she went looking for him and climbed on him to apologize and tell him the news. He became excited and hopeful that he could now get his woman's time and attention again. He started planning a fun Friday date night. They agreed to go to dinner at six so they could get in a Salsa class. He needed some personal attention and knew that the class would get them both ready to spend the night in each other's arms.

Victor called again to say goodnight and Valerie took his call. When she hung up Jefferson asked, "Being at the hospital together today wasn't enough? He's calling you every night like he's your man."

Valerie shook her head no. "He is definitely not my man. He just wanted to make sure I got home okay."

Jefferson quickly replied, "Then you should tell him that I am here when you get home so he doesn't have to do that." Valerie never commented. She had never told Victor that she was living with Jefferson. Nikki was the only Mason who knew.

On Thursday, Valerie came home from work and took a nap in the afternoon because she was so tired. Her phone never stopped ringing, between Nikki and Victor and Viveca getting her input on the questions they had about Vincent's insurance and personal preferences on setting up his house for recovery, to the rest of the family members checking in. She was happy to be done with the hospital visits, and Viveca and Victor were leaving on Sunday so life could get back to normal. They changed the medical directive to Nikki and Viveca since they were likely to be able to get to Houston to Vincent the fastest.

Valerie went to her condo on Friday to clean and check her mail. Victor had convinced Nikki to have a welcome home barbecue for Vincent on Saturday, before he and his sister left on Sunday. He called Valerie to ask her to invite Stan and Richard and the family members who had been calling about Vincent. Then he dropped the bomb: would she bring her specialties: potato salad, baked beans, and peach cobbler?

To Valerie that sounded like typical Victor. She always cooked for him when he was in town.

But she wasn't a Mason anymore so she wasn't so sure how it would look to the family, and especially to Jefferson. She said yes, deciding that it was her farewell to the Mason clan since her departure from the family had been abrupt when she put Vincent out. She made sure Victor understood that Jefferson was coming to the party too. She wanted Jefferson to get to know the family and this would be a perfect time. And she wanted him to see that she had no feelings for Vincent.

Victor was snarky but pretended to be playful. "I guess that's okay. Are you sure he can handle being around all of us Mason's? You know we are very territorial about our Valerie. I might have to show him how Mason men love you. He might not be able to handle it."

She admonished him. "Stop playing. You know I'm a Mason in name only now. And behave on Saturday with Jefferson." Victor said he was making no promises. She hung up to create her grocery list and go to the store. She realized Jefferson might not be so happy about the her cooking for the barbecue, but hoped that since he was going too, he would not be angry.

Valerie called Jefferson about the barbeque and her request that he go with her. He was irritated. "Why would I want to do that? Why do you want to go? And cook all that food for them? Can't Nikki and Viveca do that since Vincent is at home? The Mason's have had your attention all week and I'm sure they will want more before too long. Why can't I have you this weekend? That was the plan." She agreed, but asked for this one more day. "Besides, you will see them from time to time because of Nikki, this is a good time to get to know more of them. Please."

Jefferson reluctantly said yes. At least they would spend the day together, and as he had often heard from his dad, "keep your friends close and your enemies closer." What he found out though, before they hung up, was that their Friday night date had to be cancelled so Valerie could go to the grocery store. By the time she got home she was exhausted and didn't even want to watch a movie together.

Jefferson was disappointed but tried to make the best of the evening. He turned her phone off then ran a bath for her with candles, bubble bath, and soft music, and gave her the kind of therapeutic massage she gave him the first week they were together. It helped relax her so much that she was able to get ten hours of good sleep then get up early on Saturday to prepare the food while Jefferson was at the family meeting.

Steven asked about Nikki at the family meeting. Jefferson asked that they get through the next few days of Vincent getting settled in at home. He reminded Steven that they needed an update on where things stood with him and Ann. Steven was ready to give the report but Jefferson had to go so they agreed to meet the next week.

Chapter Thirty

When Jefferson got home Saturday from the family meeting, Valerie was in the kitchen wrapping the food so it would sit in the back of the car without spilling or turning over. When she was ready to go, he pulled her into his arms and gave her some deep tongue kisses like the first night she came to his house.

"What was that for?" she asked, surprised.

"I just want you to remember that you are Team Ware before you get sucked back into the Mason orbit today."

He took a moment to make his feelings known. "You do know that Victor has been using every excuse he can to talk to you every night and be with you every chance possible? I'm afraid he is getting into your head, manipulating you to keep hanging around. What's his game plan? That you would be with him now since he is obviously still in love with you? Or if not him, maybe he could help you get back with Vincent so that at least one of the Mason men would still have you?"

Valerie was defensive. "Victor is being Victor. He has always been friendly, and we hung out a lot when he came to town, especially if Vincent had to work. He always asked me to cook these dishes for him. I am using this occasion to say a final goodbye to Vincent, Victor, and the whole Mason family."

Jefferson's reply was very curt before he walked away. "There will never be a goodbye to this family until you are willing to let go. I don't think you are there yet." Valerie was shocked and had no reply. She didn't have much to say to him for the rest of the day, insulted that he thought she was being naive. He was upset that she was being gullible, walking straight into Victor's trap.

The party was scheduled to start at three so Jefferson and Valerie were a little early, perfect for getting all the food inside and set up. Jefferson then went to Vincent to say hello since it was his home. He would be confined to bed during the festivities, not moving around the house or patio so as not to put any weight on his leg.

"Hey man. Remember me? From the restaurant with Valerie? I'm Jefferson. Glad to see you on the mend. I know you're happy to be home."

Vincent was surprised to see him, but responded, "Yes, I remember you. And yes, I am very happy to be home. Thanks."

Jefferson noticed his surprise and asked, "You look surprised to see me. I guess no one told you that I was coming. Are you okay with me being here? Valerie told me that I was invited, and I wanted to see Nikki. Haven't seen her since she got here on Sunday."

Vincent's reply was brief again. "Sure, its okay, it's all good. Let me ask you something: are you serious about being with Valerie? Are you planning to marry her?"

Jefferson's voice was firm and he gave Vincent the 'Ware stare.' "I am very serious about her as I believe she is about me. We plan to get married as soon as she is free to do so." Jefferson was stating facts, not trying to take a jab at Vincent.

"Hmm. I see," was all Vincent could say before Stan walked in the room. He and Richard were going to move Vincent's bed to the living room so Vincent could be out by the family and festivities. Jefferson offered to help but they said they didn't need him so he went in search of Valerie and Nikki.

Nikki was getting dressed when Jefferson and her mom came so this was her first time seeing him. She was excited and gave him a big hug, letting everyone know of her approval of him for her mom.

Valerie was gracious, introducing Jefferson as her fiancé as she walked around the house. Each one of the family members would look from Jefferson to Vincent to Valerie and back to Jefferson, saying hello, but clearly disappointed that Valerie and Vincent were not getting back together.

Stan and Richard were very friendly to Jefferson. They were able to bond over sports and talk about Houston back in the day since all three were natives.

The Mason's spent a lot of time talking about events when Vincent, Victor, and Viveca were children, when Vincent and Valerie met and got married, and when Nikki was growing up. Jefferson asked a few questions but really had nothing to contribute and they soon stopped trying to explain to him who the other family members and friends were that they talked about.

He noticed how Victor was always close to Valerie, whether standing or sitting. He even tried to feed Valerie some fruit from his plate but she pulled her head back and pushed his hand away. Jefferson was holding his breath when he saw that. Feeding a woman or man was a very personal, sexy move, and he did not want to see Valerie open her mouth to anyone except him.

Victor was very touchy feely with her too, always under the guise of playing and joking around. Valerie was often heard laughing and saying her favorite line: "Stop Victor. You play too much."

Jefferson began to feel like an intruder. Nikki noticed how quiet he became and went over to talk with him when she took a break from serving dessert. "I'm glad to see you Daddy J! Very happy that you are here and willing to establish a relationship with my family. I don't want you to be uncomfortable around them and they need to get to know how great you are. I hope we can do more days like this after you and mom get married." Jefferson smiled at her and said, "I'll do what I can because we are all your family now. But I have a feeling that not everybody will be happy like you are about me and your mom being together." She gave him a hug and assured him, "Don't worry, I've got your back."

Just then, they both heard Victor talking to Valerie and Nikki realized that her uncle had been monopolizing her mom's time all afternoon. She said quietly to Jefferson, "Don't let these Mason's get under your skin. They love my mom and don't want to let her go so they are very territorial. He's harmless, always playing with my mom like that. My dad usually ignored him until he got on his nerves. Then he pulled the "big brother do what I say" on Victor and made him leave her alone. Don't get upset with her. She loves you now so give them a minute to get used to you." Jefferson thanked her, knowing that Victor was not going to leave Valerie alone on his own.

Vincent watched Jefferson around Valerie all afternoon. He noticed that Jefferson was attentive to Valerie, but confident enough to let her move around and visit with the Mason family without him being at her side every moment. His brother, on the other hand, was being a bit too pesty with Valerie like he always was. That was not his problem anymore so he sat back to watch and see if Jefferson would check him.

When Valerie started cleaning up behind the other family members, taking plates and glasses to the kitchen, Jefferson called her over to him. "You are looking very much like the lady of the house instead of a guest. First, you were serving people's plates, now you are cleaning up. Why don't you sit here with me and let the Mason family do that." It was a statement, not a question. She looked in his eyes and saw that he was serious so she sat with him.

Jefferson started to think that Valerie was liking the Mason reunion more than maybe she even realized. He knew it was time to go so he asked her to say her goodbyes. She started to protest, then decided she didn't want another fight or another night not speaking or sleeping together so she got up and he did too.

They made their way to Viveca and Victor to say "safe travels." When Victor tried to hug Valerie, Jefferson leaned over to say, so only Victor could hear, "I think you have hugged and touched and played with her enough. I've got this now." They had another "man to man" look and Victor backed off, pretending to need to see a cousin who was out on the patio.

About halfway home, Jefferson took the opportunity to ask, "You know he's still in love with you? Victor. And we already know that Vincent was having second thoughts about divorcing you, so both Mason men want you. You said you have not seen Victor in a couple of years but you two have talked. Has he ever mentioned his feelings for you?"

She hesitated to respond, then finally said, "Victor always joked about it through the years, saying that I married the wrong brother and he would be waiting if I ever figured it out for myself. I never took him seriously. I thought he was just saying stuff to get under Vincent's skin. After I started divorce proceedings, he called to check on me but I never thought what he was saying was his way of hitting on me. Maybe he was waiting for the divorce. Honestly, I was never attracted to him like that because he was such a player and never wanted to settle down. That would have been a mess and I'm glad I never entertained the thought. How did you know?"

"What do the young people say, "Game knows Game"? I could see it immediately when he hugged and kissed you at the airport when he first arrived."

Valerie got her chance to ask, "So that was the look that passed between you two at the airport? Game acknowledging Game?"

"Yes actually. It's a man thing and nothing he or I will probably ever talk about. I was hoping that he would be able to move on finally since you are with me and will not be reaching out for him. After seeing him today though, always close by you, touching you, only looking at you when he's talking, even trying to feed you, I think he might be working up to shooting his shot for real. Just be careful V. Don't get fooled by his cover of playfulness.

"I'm not going to worry about his intentions. I am, however, concerned about your response to him. Are we good?" Jefferson wanted to hear some kind of affirmation from Valerie that she was still on the Ware team. Valerie said "Of course," to Jefferson's question, but she became quiet, nervous about how Victor acted around her and making a mental note to keep her distance.

He suggested, "Let's skip Game Day so we can spend a romantic Sunday in bed together. I miss you. It's my turn to need you. I want to be inside you." Valerie smiled in response but when they got home and in bed, he tried to get close to her. She turned away from Jefferson, claiming she was tired. Jefferson knew the signs. She was restless with something on her mind. He wondered if Valerie had started feeling distant from him, distracted even, very focused on the Mason's and not on him or their relationship anymore.

Valerie was thinking of all the times she and Victor had spoken since she and Vincent separated, and then the times they had been together the last week. Jefferson was right. Victor *was* always physically close to her, touching her, looking at her. She enjoyed his company because he was fun and family. Had she been giving him signals that he might now have a chance? Did she see him differently now that she had a more fun person in Jefferson to compare to what Victor could offer? The thoughts were a little scary to her.

She loved Jefferson and Victor, believing that the love for each one was different. Victor was a relative, a brother-in-law. Jefferson was her man, her love. Now she is wondering if she was harboring feelings deep down for Victor through the years and just didn't know how not to cause a scandal. She was glad that Victor was leaving and she could re-focus on Jefferson and getting Vincent to sign the papers.

Chapter Thirty-One

There was no romantic Sunday for Jefferson and Valerie so he ordered food in preparation for Game Day. Jefferson and Valerie gave Jeannette and Steven the update on Vincent's progress and the news that he was home recuperating. Steven then asked for Nikki's number. He was happy about Mr. Mason being on the mend, yet concerned about what Nikki was still having to go through with her dad, especially since her uncle and aunt were leaving that day. He was ready to talk about what had been going on with him and Ann, and how things had changed. Mostly he was excited because he thought he had to wait another month or two to see Nikki and now he could see her in a day or two.

Jefferson was protective. "Let us talk to Nikki and get back to you. We need to know what's going on with you and Ann. Maybe you still need to wait."

Steven reported good news. "Ann has found a house within fifteen minutes of our house and Jason's school. She said she likes the area and wanted to stay close to us as well as her favorite stores, bank, and library. I talked to mom and she liked my idea to give her the down payment as our appreciation for all that she has done for us. We also agreed that she would have Jason over to spend the night sometimes. He is still her godson after all and a clean break would not be right for either of them. I have arranged for after school care and can now leave in time to pick Jason up every day."

There was one thing he wanted to ask: "If, in an emergency, can you or mom step in so that I don't have to call Ann?" They both agreed, and even Valerie said she would be happy to be included since she was home more than either of them. They all looked to Jeannette for approval since she was the one with an issue with Valerie. She approved. Anything for her son and grandson. Besides, she didn't think Valerie was out to do physical harm to Jason or Steven, or any of them actually.

Steven heaved a sigh of relief to see them all smile at the changes that he described. He was also happy to share that, "Jason is adjusting well to it being just the two of us and learning to do laundry, cook together, and shop for groceries. It's like I'm learning to be a dad all over again and Jason is happy to be my sidekick. He's more mature than I ever noticed before." He looked happy with his new level of involvement as a dad.

Valerie asked what his thoughts were now about Nikki.

"It's been a few weeks now and so much has changed, but I still want to get to know her. It will be a lot easier since she is in town. That is if she is open to me calling her?" Steven realized that Nikki might have moved on or be too busy with her dad to have any time for him but he wanted to talk to her to find out.

Valerie looked at Jefferson and Jeannette to see if they had any objections but they both shrugged, leaving it to her to decide. She went into the bedroom to call Nikki, telling her about Steven and Ann deciding to go their separate ways and Steven wanting her number. She didn't tell her all that Steven had said, deferring to him to fill in the details of his story. Nikki was definitely still interested. Valerie walked back into the kitchen texting Steven the number he had been hoping for along with a request to be gentle with her baby. When he looked at his phone, Steven smiled and hugged Valerie, whispering his promise to do so.

Dinner was chicken and trimmings from one of the fast food restaurants so they ate and relaxed into just enjoying each other and the food. After everyone was gone, Jefferson asked Valerie how she was feeling about Steven calling Nikki. She was satisfied with all of that Steven had told them, but repeated her comment from before: "I'm still concerned about them becoming family because of us then adding dating to the mix, but as you said, they are grown so let them work it out. I can do that."

Jefferson was not so sure any more about he and Valerie being an "us" but he did not comment. He needed to see signs that Valerie was again focused on him and them getting married. They had not discussed it since the first night they went to the hospital. From that day until this one, Valerie's entire focus was on her old family.

Chapter Thirty-Two

Jefferson asked Valerie about her schedule for the week and whether they could go away for a few days to New York. He was determined to keep fighting for her attention. She said yes, but her response was still missing the enthusiasm she usually had for him. He was talking about where they would stay and what plays they might see when her phone rang. It was Victor, letting her know he had made it home. Jefferson took her phone out of her hand, hit the mute button, and asked her to hang up so they could talk. She took her phone back and waved him away, saying, "I'll only be a minute." She went into the den to give Victor her attention. He could hear her laughing and joking with him. When they hung up, she headed for bed, chuckling to herself about something Victor had said, forgetting that she and Jefferson were in the middle of a conversation.

Jefferson decided to go to bed too since that was the only place he could get close to her. He could tell she was already half asleep so he whispered his usual nightly wish, "dream of us," in her ear and tried to pull her over to him to get into their usual position. She pulled away.

When he moved over to spoon with her and put his arm around her, she started mumbling, "Stop Victor." As soon as she said it, she became fully alert. Her body stiffened, her eyes flew open, and her heart started beating fast. Did Jefferson hear what she said? Did he know that she was half-asleep?

She got her answers immediately when Jefferson froze with his hand on her arm then pulled it back, rolled over away from her and out of bed, putting on his jeans and a tee shirt. He went to the den, trying to decide what to do. He had had enough of Vincent and Victor, but clearly Valerie wanted more of them. She enjoyed being a Mason, and this week of her immersion back into family business and the barbeque confirmed that to him. She followed him, saying, "I'm sorry. I didn't mean to say that. I was half asleep."

He walked out to the garage and shut the door in her face. She opened the door and he gave her such a look of hurt and anger that she could not speak. He spoke to her and his tone was cold and abrasive. "You need to leave me alone right now. You had no time for me tonight when I was trying to talk with you about a trip together so don't bother now." She went back to bed but never went to sleep and he stayed in the garage, sitting in his car wondering how he would get past this bad turn of the relationship.

In the morning while his coffee brewed, he went to the garage for all of Valerie's travel bags she had used to bring her clothes to Jefferson's house: two large suitcases and two carryon roller bags. While Valerie was in the shower, he put them on the bed, open and ready to be filled. When she walked out of the bathroom, and saw all of her suitcases she knew what that meant. The message was crystal clear.

Jefferson was in the kitchen scrolling through his phone when she ran to him with tears in her eyes and apologies still on her lips. "Please don't do this. I made one mistake. Can't you forgive me?" Jefferson looked up at her. His voice went up an octave as he let her know that, "As far as I'm concerned, you were awake enough to know that you said the wrong thing so how asleep were you really? I do not appreciate you even thinking about, much less dreaming about, another man in our bed, especially one I told you had feelings for you. And to reject me with another man's name on your lips? I don't need another sign to tell me our time is up. Go back to your Mason cocoon and resume the life you clearly miss."

He looked at her beautiful face and hair, and down then up her body before responding quietly. "Your feelings have clearly changed about me. About us. I understand. I can't compete with thirty years of family so I will not try any more. Be happy with whichever Mason man you decide to be with, since both of them want you. I can understand why. You are a fabulous woman, and I'm glad to have known you.

"When you are done packing, I will take your bags to the car. Make sure you get everything that you brought over. If you need more luggage, you can have mine. I can buy more." He put his head back down to scroll on his phone. She was dismissed.

She sat for a minute, looking at him with tears falling silently from her eyes. She got up slowly from the table and made her way back to the bedroom to pack. The one thing she had learned about Jefferson was that he was a man who meant what he said. He meant it when he said he wanted her very soon after their meeting, when he told Jeannette she had to deal with whatever he chose to do with the property when he and Valerie got married, and she knew it today when he made sure she knew she had to leave. Nothing came to mind to say to him that might make him change his mind so she got to work.

Valerie cried the whole time she packed, starting with bathroom toiletries first, then the clothes in drawers, then everything on hangers. She was hoping he would come in the room while she was packing so that she could try pleading with him again but he didn't.

She finally realized how absorbed she had been with the Masons and it had nothing to do with helping Nikki. She was enjoying the attention that she used to get when she was Vincent's wife. That led to her being easily persuaded to fall into Victor's trap, curious to see if he really was the fun brother that she had missed by being with Vincent.

This was her wake-up call. She knew she had to go, but in her heart of hearts, she believed Jefferson was the man for her and she was the woman he was meant to be with. The question was whether he knew that too despite this horrible turn of events.

When she walked back in the kitchen, he asked if she was ready to go. She could only nod her head, knowing that if she spoke she would start crying again.

Jefferson made sure everything was in the car then took the garage door opener off her visor and used it to open the garage door. They looked at each other one last time before she pulled out.

He closed the door down before Valerie was out of the driveway, went back in the house and de-activated her code. After changing the linen and taking a long hot shower, Jefferson called Jeannette so she and Steven would not come over for Game Day or be worried, then went to bed and slept into the evening, waking up only to go to the bathroom, get a beer, and check voicemail messages.

His ego and heart were not just bruised, they were shattered. He clearly didn't know how to pick a woman. Both of the ones he chose made it clear he was a pit-stop in their lives, they had other agendas, lives that did not include him.

His phone rang several times on Sunday night but he refused to answer it. When he listened to the messages, they were from Steven, his friend Zeke, and one from Nikki looking for her mother who was not answering her phone.

On Monday, Jefferson gave Ron the week off with pay so he could keep busy and not have time to think of Valerie. He wanted all of the assignments and everything else he needed to do so that he got home late and tired and went right to bed. He didn't know how long that would work, but it was a start to healing.

Chapter Thirty-Three

Nikki's Monday morning call to her mother started out upbeat. She was happy to report that she had spoken with Steven and he had given her details of the changes in his life. They had agreed to talk on the phone until she got her dad situated at home and on a schedule, then maybe he could come visit, or they could even go on a date when Uncle Victor or Aunt Viveca came back.

The quiet way Valerie responded told Nikki that something was terribly wrong. Valerie was trying too hard to sound normal and kept saying everything was fine, but daughters know their mothers. Valerie never explained why she didn't answer her phone the night before. Nikki gave her an update on Vincent and they hung up.

Nikki worried for the rest of the day. Even her dad asked her what was wrong, especially since she had been so happy after Steven's call. She told him she was just deciding on how much FMLA to take before she called her boss so she was thinking through projects and assignments. He did not believe her.

On Tuesday morning, Valerie talked with the same strained voice as on Monday but their call was cut short by a knock on Valerie's condo door which confirmed for Nikki that Valerie was not at Jefferson's house. Nikki was more firm in her questions to her mom when she called back.

"Tell me mom, what's happened? Where is Daddy J? Why are you at the condo—is something wrong there that you have to be at your place? Why do you sound so strange? I'm getting scared that you're not telling me something I need to know so please tell me the truth. Are you sick? What is wrong?"

Valerie finally told Nikki about her calling out Victor's name in her half sleep and what led up to that and how Jefferson had ended their relationship. Valerie cried softly and said she was just sad and would feel better soon, especially when her lawyer filed the papers to speed up the divorce. Nikki was sad for her mother and cried too. She loved Daddy J and saw how happy her mother was with him. She told her mother she was coming to be with her on Friday for the weekend because Aunt Viveca would be up to stay with Vincent. No arguments. Valerie protested but was secretly glad. She needed a hug, and if she couldn't get it from Jefferson, Nikki's would be perfect.

Valerie spent the rest of the week holed up in her apartment, staring out her windows but not looking at anything. Her focus was on what had happened with Jefferson and what she was going to do about Vincent and now Victor.

On Friday night, Nikki and Checkers showed up at the condo with dinner, ready to have some girl time. It felt strange for them to be back together at the Valerie's place after the Memorial Day weekend when they were all at Jefferson's house. Valerie wasn't crying anymore but was still sad. It was date night, Salsa and spending the night at the condo. She wanted to call Jefferson but decided against it. She thought he needed some time to miss her.

The weekend with Nikki was good. They went out to eat, walk the *Galleria*, and browse at the *Black Arts Festival*. Valerie was kept busy so she would not be sad all day. At night, they talked about men and what Valerie wanted to do about Jefferson. Valerie talked tough, saying he just needed time to calm down and realize it was an honest mistake after being with the Mason's, especially Victor, all day.

Nikki gently explained why she did not agree, saying that Uncle Vic had always been overbearing and her dad always had to check him to keep him in line. Valerie had never noticed, never heard Vincent say anything to Victor about her. Nikki also expressed her belief that Jefferson was a man's man and he would probably not come for her since she was calling out another man's name in bed. She went back to her dad's leaving Valerie with a lot to think about.

On Sunday, Valerie told her sister about calling out Victor's name to Jefferson. Stephanie wanted to fuss at Valerie for letting Victor get in her head after all these years. She had learned not to kick a person when he or she is down so she did not say anything that would upset Valerie. She did, however, schedule a trip to Houston for the following weekend to spend time with her. She also hoped there was a way to finally meet Jefferson but did not get her hopes up.

Valerie spent the week until her sister arrived really thinking about what Nikki said and what Jefferson really meant to her. Victor called every night, and when Valerie finally asked him what he wanted with her, why he was calling so much all of a sudden, he confessed.

"I always thought you were the prettiest girl in high school, but I was not that confident even though I was a jock and girls were coming on to me. I got my swag in college and honed it my first few years working. When Vincent brought you home to meet the family I was hoping you two were just friends and I could take you out on dates, but he said you guys had been dating for a while and he was going to ask you to marry him. Biggest heartbreak for me.

"I have spent all the years you were married hating that I didn't speak up because I knew you first. And hating that he got to you before I could find you and we could get together. I was always hoping that you would see through my jokes, and notice how I was always standing or sitting close to you so we could figure out a way to be together. It never happened. It probably would have been messy in the family if it had, but I thought you were worth the risk. Now you are about to marry another man. I knew this was my last chance to get with you so I went a little overboard this past week, especially at the barbeque, to get your attention. That didn't work huh?"

Valerie told him emphatically, "No." She asked him why he never got married. He admitted, "I never wanted to be tied down to one woman because I am admittedly a work-a-holic and selfish. I didn't want to make room in my life for a wife and definitely didn't want children. Hook-ups and casual affairs have been my way of life. The women I spent the most time with always got a nice parting gift so they were happy."

"So you would not have even married me?" Valerie was curious.

"Oh, who knows? Probably would have had a long-term relationship with you though. I would have taken good care of you. You are definitely the one that got away."

Valerie ended that call very disappointed at the kind of man Victor described. She was glad she never thought about being with him while married and now was sorry to have wasted time thinking of what might have been with him.

Chapter Thirty-Four

Somehow, Valerie and Jefferson both started marking time in a similar way: the number of weeks after the break-up. She was easing into a post-Jefferson life and trying to figure out what that would look like. He was counting the weeks it would take for the hurt to go away.

Week One of the breakup. Jefferson was kept very busy with a number of work calls each day and the paperwork they had to fill out each night for the tenants files, documenting the service they received. Valerie put a full court press on her attorney to talk to Vincent's attorney about getting the divorce papers signed, no more delays. In addition, she shopped for a dress for Lillian and Max's party. Retail therapy always helped her with stress.

Steven called his mother and Jefferson and asked to meet at his mom's house on Wednesday evening. Jeannette asked why Valerie was not there. She could tell something was wrong with her brother on their morning calls that week. His conversations were brief, dry. She knew he was sad about something, but when she asked if he was okay or what was wrong, Jefferson only said, "Mind your business."

Jeannette and Steven both knew something big had happened but didn't push. They focused on Steven and the reason for the meeting.

He reported good news. "The closing on Ann's house is next week. I need a favor: help me get Ann situated in her house. She chose a small three bedroom cottage style flat that is a bit of a fixer. The roof and foundation are good, but it is in need of some painting, the kitchen cabinets and floor replaced, and some small repairs and changes. I was hoping you could help me with that, Unc. Plus she has no furniture so she wants you, mom, to go shopping with her since you have such a good eye for decorating."

Jeannette and Jefferson were both happy to help. Jefferson was especially excited because it would give him something to do to keep him busy and tired so that he wouldn't miss Valerie so much. He just had to get through this first week, then Ann would close on her house and they could get started.

Jeannette kept watching Jefferson throughout the evening, noticing he was attentive during the conversation, but rather quiet, saying only, "Of course I'll help," when Steven asked. She finally asked about Valerie. "Hey big brother. What's really going on with you and Ms. Valerie? You've been real evasive on the phone in the mornings when I have asked about her, saying she's fine, but now that I see you I know something bad has happened. You look like all the wind has been knocked out of your sail. What is it? Did she cheat on you? Did you finally figure out she really does want all your money? What happened?" She was trying to goad him into telling them what was going on.

Jefferson's response was the usual, "Mind your business." Steven took a good look at his uncle and saw what his mom was talking about. He had not seen his uncle look so somber and understood immediately that it was heartbreak, not health or business issues. The tone of the evening changed so Jefferson was ready to go and Steven needed to get home to Jason and get him ready for bed. He was with Ann while Steven had the meeting with his mom and uncle.

On the way to their cars, Steven took a moment to say to Jefferson, "I don't know what happened, but if you ever want to talk, I'm here for you. I know you love Ms. Valerie so if you split up it was not good. I know it's not the exact situation, but I don't want you to do like I did after Carla died and withdraw from life for too long. Anything I can do, I will. If you don't feel like dealing with Ann's house, it's ok. I can get some of my guys from work to help. I asked you because you taught me everything I know and I like it when we work together but no pressure."

Steven tried not to think of how he would ever get with Nikki if Ms. Valerie and Uncle Jeff were not together. He decided he had enough to think about for the next few weeks and hoped it would work itself out. In the meantime, he would keep talking to Nikki on the phone, updating her on the progress with Ann's home and eventually getting a date with her.

Jefferson smiled a sad smile at Steven then replied, "I'll be okay. And I will enjoy helping with Ann's house. It's just what I need right now to keep my mind occupied. Thanks." Jefferson wasn't quite ready to go home so he drove to the Fifth Ward to check out the next area where he was thinking of buying property. Anything to keep from going to his empty house too soon.

Chapter Thirty-Five

Week Two after the breakup. Jefferson split all the jobs that came in with Ron even though Ron did not need his help. He was still feeling too anxious and needed to stay busy. Ann was closing on her house later in the week so they would get started on remodeling for her on Saturday after the family meeting.

Fortified by Nikki's visit, Valerie worked her regular hours then prepared for Stephanie to come on Friday. Her retail therapy continued during the week as she searched for an anniversary gift for Lillian and Max.

The sisters thoroughly enjoyed each other over the weekend. They had a pajama party like they did in their teens and tried different make-up, different hairstyles to go with Valerie's new party dress, braided each other's hair, ate pizza and popcorn, watched movies, and talked about men in general and Jefferson in particular.

Stephanie encouraged Valerie not to give up on him, saying it sounded like he was perfect for her and maybe with the divorce papers in hand he might be more open to talking, or even getting back together. Most important, Stephanie emphasized, stay away from the Mason men. Valerie smiled and said that was part of her plan, she just had to get the divorce papers and find the right opportunity to meet with Jefferson.

Ann closed on her house and the whole Ware family converged on it at noon on Saturday, right after the family meeting. They walked through room by room, and even Jason was enjoying picking his room and talking about what color he wanted his walls and where his toys would go. They made lists of what needed to be done for the inside and front and back yards, what they had to purchase to fix things up, what furniture was needed, and the schedule of days they were going to work. Jefferson was thrilled to have so much to do to keep him occupied. Nights without Valerie were not getting easier.

Ann gave Jefferson a credit card for the materials since he would be shopping while Steven was at work. He and Steven got keys to the house so they could come and go when they had time while she continued to stay with Steven and look after Jason until her house was complete. Jefferson and Steven first installed an alarm then went shopping right away and brought in the paint and supplies they would need. Jefferson said he would bring his equipment and do most of the work during the week since he had more time, then save the big tasks for Saturdays and Sundays when Steven was off work. They cancelled Game Day until Ann's house was complete.

After Stephanie left on Sunday, Valerie realized that Jefferson was not coming for her so she left a voicemail message for him at 10pm. It was the time they usually headed for bed even if they stayed up a while to read or make love. "I am truly sorry and hope that one day you will forgive me. I love you and only you. Dream of us."

Jefferson also heard from Stephanie while she was at the Houston airport. He didn't know anyone in the area code that showed up on his phone and had let the call go to voicemail too. "I've done all I can do to help Val get through this weekend. Don't know if it means anything to you, but she is hurting. Crushed. I hope you will one day forgive her. If you're ever in the Bay area, give me a call. I'll buy you dinner and we can get to know each other. You will always be my brother-in-law even if you don't marry my sister. But I hope you will."

Valerie called again Monday night. He could hear that she had been crying but she was trying to sound strong. "I miss you so much. Don't you miss me too? I am just a phone call away. I would love to hear your voice. You know how I love your voice. Or even better, just come over. Use your key and let me wake up in your arms. Well ok. Good night. Dream of us."

On Tuesday night, there was an update: "I spoke with Vincent today and he has agreed to sign the divorce papers. He said he could see clearly at the hospital and at his house that I would not entertain anything else he had to say. He has come to terms with the fact that I have moved on, and he thinks you would take good care of me. I don't know what you said to him at the barbeque, but thank you. I hope that is good news to you. I love you and I miss you. Dream of us."

The rest of the week Jefferson worked at Ann's and did not to listen to any more of the nightly messages from Valerie. Her voice was distracting, keeping him in his feelings for her. He didn't erase them though. He knew there would come a time that he would want to hear them.

Chapter Thirty-Six

Week Three after the breakup. Ann's house came together quickly over the two weeks, mostly because Jefferson worked every night until almost midnight, still avoiding being home alone. He painted every room, replaced baseboards and floors, hung chandeliers and other lighting after having the house rewired, and he and Steven put in the new kitchen cabinets and appliances. He oversaw his company putting in new landscaping and had her house added to the grass cutting schedule, and had a company install a new fence so that her back yard was enclosed. She and Jeannette had all the furniture delivered and on the following Saturday, Ann moved in.

The whole Ware/Jackson family was there, some of Ann's family, and even Carla's parents who considered Ann another daughter, came over to help. Everybody paired up and took a room, making the beds, setting up the kitchen and bathrooms, putting furniture in the right places so by the end of the day it looked like she had lived there for a long time. Ann was thrilled and very grateful and had a full summer holiday style meal catered—ribs, chicken, brats, corn on the cob, potato and fruit salads, Cole slaw, soft drinks, beer, cakes, pies, and cookies. She asked Steven if they could have a minute to talk before he and Jason left.

"Thank you Steven. For allowing me to live with you and help raise Jason, honoring my promise to Carla, and for all that you and your family have done to set me up in this house. I understand that we were not meant to be together so I wish you well with Nikki or whomever you date or marry. I just don't want things to be awkward between us going forward because I do love Jason and want to see him whenever he wants to come over and as often as you need me to keep him. I love you both. You are my family and I never want that to change."

Steven was very happy to hear her say those things because he didn't want things to be awkward either. He just wasn't sure when or how to say it to her. "I do love you Ann. You are my sister and my son's godmother forever. Thank you for loving us and taking care of us, for getting me through the darkest time of my life and making my son a great, loving kid. Carla would be proud and thankful too. I hope you find the man who can appreciate you and love you the way you want. If you ever need anything, just let me know."

Steven left Ann's house feeling relieved and free to explore his dating life. Now he was eager to reach out to Nikki, but his Uncle Jeff was still having a hard time. The opportunity to fully connect with Nikki was looking bleak. He decided to settle in to his new household situation with Jason and see what happened. He didn't want to date anyone else so he would wait.

Jefferson noticed that since he had been working so hard over the past three weeks he had worked through a lot of his sadness about losing Valerie. He was able to go home and relax. She still called every night at 10pm, but now it was bittersweet. He still loved her and missed her, but the sting of losing her was not as bad. Maybe because he knew she still missed him and that was comforting. Was he healing? Or just fooling himself? His love didn't dissipate in three weeks. Maybe he was just getting used to her being gone and at some point he would be ready to date again.

With Vincent's signature on the divorce papers, Valerie's lawyer filed the papers with the court and her marriage was finally dissolved. She started thinking of when and how she would tell Jefferson. She knew she could not announce it on the phone on one of her nightly calls, and she had not seen him since that Sunday morning when she left his house. In the meantime, she kept up her nightly calls to him and went back to her routine before Jefferson: working, lunch with friends, reading, being out at museums and art shows.

Her college friend without benefits, Curtis, called to say that he was coming to Houston and asked Valerie for lunch on the following Saturday. She was always happy to hang out with him and thought that maybe she could talk to him about how to reach out to Jefferson, getting a man's perspective. Curtis always said she was the one who got away, but he was happily married and happy to be a "brother" to Valerie. He always gave good advice, even about her divorcing Vincent. He believed it was long overdue.

Chapter Thirty-Seven

Week Four after the breakup. Jeannette was happy that Ann was settled into her new house then realized that Steven would want to date Nikki. She noticed that Jefferson was still rather quiet and Valerie had not been around so she decided not to mention Valerie and hope that his time with her was really over. If that was true, she figured Steven would not have an opportunity to date Nikki. She didn't know that Steven and Nikki had talked and agreed it would be awkward to date when Jefferson and Valerie were not seeing each other.

Jeannette invited Ann to a girl's weekend of eating and drinking in New Orleans, her final thank you gift to Ann for loving and taking care of her family. They planned to leave on Friday and return late on Sunday.

When the two women went away, Jefferson and Jeannette's cousin Doris called on Friday about coming from Tulsa, Oklahoma early on Saturday. Doris, Jeannette, and Jefferson were like brother and sisters. Their mothers were sisters and very close, so of course the children grew up at each other's houses every week. Since Jeannette was out of town, she was staying with Jefferson.

The purpose of her visit was to check on her family home because renters had moved out the weekend before and she needed to assess any damages and get it ready for the next tenants. She was even thinking of selling it because she was tired of the responsibility, especially since she lived out of town now.

Doris and Jefferson went to check out the house and then to lunch to discuss him buying it to add to his portfolio. She noticed he was unusually quiet so she asked what was going on with him. He knew she would keep his confidence so he told her about Valerie.

Doris was happy that he had found someone to love and at the same time sad for him that it hadn't worked out. She agreed it was hard to fight family and a thirty-year marriage, even with cheating involved. When he told her about Jeannette's attitude with Valerie about the property, Doris shook her head. "I see she hasn't changed. Always thinking "me and mine" and five steps ahead. Guess that's how she was able to manage as a single mother and why she's so good at her job. Do you want me to talk to her?" Jefferson shook his head no, so she did not press or make any further comments.

They went to *The Capital Grille* for lunch. He had the grilled ribeye sandwich and house salad, she had the miniature tenderloin sandwiches with cole slaw. They talked about the family and looked at pictures of Steven and Jason and Doris' kids and grandchildren on their cell phones. They agreed that he would buy the house to keep it in the family.

As they were finishing lunch, Jefferson's anxiety level increased dramatically. The hair on his arms stood up. He sensed something, not sure if trouble was about to happen or if he was starting to feel sick. He couldn't figure it out but the feeling persisted. He put his fork down, pushed his plate away, and folded his hands on top of the table. He looked around the restaurant. There was no noise or unusual movement so he could not understand what was making him so suspicious. He looked toward the door to see if he could see anything happening at the host station. Nothing. The feeling did not go away.

Suddenly the door opened and Valerie walked through it looking so good his mouth watered. Her hair was loose and wild on her head and she had on a form fitted straight orange, white, and blue print dress and navy heels. She looked fabulous. Other men in the room noticed her too. She paused at the host station and a man came up behind her, putting his hand on the small of her back to guide her to their table. She stopped mid-way into the room and slowly looked around, sensing something too. She had a slight frown on her face until her eyes locked with Jefferson's. She pointed the man she was with to their table and stood for a moment, looking at Jefferson.

Jefferson watched her with a blank expression on his face as she walked over to him. She nodded to his lunch date, then put her hand in between both of his. She leaned over to kiss him on the cheek and whisper in his ear, "It's good to see you Jeff. Have you been getting my messages?" He nodded yes, inhaling her scent and loving it. Then she whispered, "The man I am with is Curtis, just a friend, like your Helen. I don't know who this lady is to you, but you and I are not done. It's time for me to come home." With that said, she kissed him on the lips, stood up, looked him in the eyes, and walked to the table where Curtis was sitting.

Doris and Jefferson sat quietly for a few minutes after Valerie left the table.

Doris was looking at Jefferson. He was looking straight ahead. Finally, Doris smiled at Jefferson and said, "I know that's got to be Valerie. Damn cuz, she's beautiful and bold. Go on and get your woman. I can go to a hotel or head on back home." Jefferson kept a straight face and said, "That won't be necessary. We can go now."

He left without looking over at Valerie. He was happy to see her, and chuckled to himself about the way she came over to the table and staked her claim on him, in front of Doris and everyone else in the restaurant, including her date, her "Helen." Damn he loved that woman. Then he was sad again because he remembered she didn't love him the way he loved her.

Chapter Thirty-Eight

Doris and Jefferson went back to his house, and for the rest of the day Doris kept saying, "Let it go. We don't get many real loves in our lives. You apparently have a good one so don't miss out by being stubborn. Call her. Go get her." Jefferson told her what he always told Jeannette, "Mind your business."

At ten pm that night, his doorbell rang. Jefferson was just coming out of the shower so he had to get dressed. He asked Doris to see who it was.

Valerie was startled to see the woman from lunch and she had on nightclothes. She started to leave then instead, turned back and asked for Jefferson to come to the door. Doris smiled and said, "Sure, just a minute," then closed the door. Valerie thought the woman was laughing at her but she didn't care. She needed one last moment with Jefferson.

Doris didn't tell him who it was, saying with a smile, "You have a visitor." He looked out the window and saw it was Valerie on the porch with an overnight bag hanging off her shoulder. Her car was on the street because his driveway was full with his truck and Doris' car. He hesitated before opening the door, trying to prepare himself for whatever she had to say.

He finally opened the door, but did not say anything to her, his face blank. She had tears falling from her eyes. "I came here thinking that it's been a month and maybe you would be ready to talk to me again and let me come home. But I see you have moved on. She must be special since she's here and you said you don't usually have women at your house." She was nodding at the car in the driveway. "So I'll just say I love you and I'm sorry and I will not bother you again."

He watched her go to her car on the street, get in and lock the door. She crossed her arms over the steering wheel and leaned forward, putting her head on her arms, crying so hard she could not drive away.

Seeing her at lunchtime made Jefferson feel the strong attachment to her again but he fought the feelings. Seeing her tonight, however, crying at his door and in her car unable to drive away, broke him.

He walked slowly out to her and knocked on the window. She rolled the window down but didn't look at him. "I'm leaving," she said softly, pleading through her tears. "I just need a minute. Please." He opened the door and pulled her out, wrapping his arms around her, holding her until she stopped crying. He took her bag out of the back seat, made sure the window was up and the car locked so they could walk together into the house. As they walked up the driveway, he told her, "The car belongs to my cousin, Doris, the woman I was having lunch with today. She is staying with me for the weekend."

Valerie was very happy to hear that, but still not sure of what was about to happen with him. Was he bringing her in to talk to work things out or tell her to leave him alone? Would she end up spending the night? Was he going to forgive her and let her move back in with him? She was not feeling quite as confident now as she had been at the restaurant, but she was going to be strong and find out. This might be her only moment to get back with him so she took a deep breath, held her head up, and walked behind him.

He walked her to the bedroom and put her bag on the bed. She sat next to it while he leaned on the dresser with his arms crossed over his chest and his legs crossed at the ankle, still looking at her but not saying anything. Finally he asked, "What is it Valerie? I heard all of your messages saying you were sorry and that you love me. How can I trust that when you called out another man's name in our bed? A man you are connected to for life through your daughter. And let's not forget that his brother, your ex-husband, still loves you too."

She reached into her bag and pulled out some papers that were stapled together and folded in three sections. She opened them to the first page and handed them to Jefferson. They were her divorce papers, signed and notarized. Her marriage was officially and finally over. She had received them over a week ago. Seeing him at the restaurant was the sign she needed to know that today was the day to let him know. He looked at them and handed them back to her.

Valerie pleaded her case, looking him directly in his eyes. "I am sorry. Truthfully, it was fun hanging out with the Mason's again, but I let that life go three years ago. The time at the hospital was like a formal goodbye to the family, one we didn't get when I kicked Vincent out. Saying Victor's name was just a fluke, a residual from saying that to him throughout the day. It was a horrible mistake and I can't say enough how sorry I am.

"This time apart has shown me that I can't live without you and I need you to forgive me. I started calling you every night so that you would not forget me and maybe my voice would help you miss me and want me back. Doris is your cousin and I am glad, but have you been seeing someone else in the last month? Just so you know, I haven't been with Victor or anyone else. I just want to be with you. I will never do anything that insensitive ever again. It is Team Ware forever for me. So will you forgive me and let me back into your life?"

He didn't answer for a minute, rubbing his face, then finally said, "How about this: let's go to bed and talk tomorrow. That is all I can give you right now. It's been a full day, a full month actually, and I need to rest and think."

She was happy to get to spend the night so she changed clothes and laid next to him in bed, hesitating about moving into their usual position. He laid on his side away from her, not wanting to risk reaching for her and hearing the wrong thing out of her mouth.

Jefferson waited for Val to fall asleep so he could ease out of bed and go into the den to think. Somehow, he knew this day would come and he would have to make a decision on whether they should resume their relationship.

She looked so good to him. He could tell that she had lost a few pounds and the dark circles he saw when she took her makeup off confirmed that she had not been sleeping well. He had not either, and he didn't that night.

By the time the sun came up, he had decided to try love with Valerie one more time, but he did not want to get married. He did not want to compete with her first marriage of thirty years or either of the Mason men finding reasons to reach out to her. They could just date and enjoy each other's company. They didn't even have to live together. It would be interesting to see if Valerie would agree to that, especially since she had suggested it before when dividing property was an issue with Jeannette. That was then. Maybe he would eventually change his mind, but the wounds were still too fresh for that to happen now.

Chapter Thirty-Nine

When Valerie woke up, she was in bed alone. She could hear Jefferson in the kitchen with Doris so she made a call to Nikki to let her know where she was, asking her not to get her hopes up yet. She and Jefferson still needed to talk.

Nikki offered her advice: "Mom, don't push him. Let him tell you what he wants when he is ready. It might take a while for him to decide so you have to be patient. He really does love you. He's hurt. And men don't process hurt the way women do. We talk to our girlfriends and dissect everything from A to Z. Men hold it in. Sometimes they drink or gamble, maybe even have a bunch of other women. Give him time."

Valerie responded softly, "Look at my daughter giving me romance advice. I'm sure you're right since you have a lot of men brother/friends and more boyfriends than I had before I got married. I'll try to be patient, but you know how I am." They laughed, knowing how impatient Valerie had always been. She knew she had to at least try what Nikki said. She definitely wanted Jefferson back. Valerie made the bed, dressed, and headed for the kitchen.

VALENTINE LOVE

Doris and Jefferson were having coffee when Valerie joined them. Doris smiled at her and said how happy she was to meet her and that she needed to give lessons on how to make bold moves to get your man. Valerie smiled hesitantly back at her then looked at Jefferson before responding. "I'm not sure that I've got him. I might have to make another bold move to seal the deal. Do you have any ideas?"

Doris looked at her cousin but directed her comments to Valerie. "Yes. Just stay here and do not leave. He's glad you're here. He can be stubborn, but he'll come around." Jefferson told her again, "Mind your business." Doris laughed saying, "She asked me. I'm just giving her a suggestion." Then she winked at Valerie and got up to get dressed and head back to Tulsa.

Valerie walked over to Jefferson and stood between his legs, pressing her body to his and her lips to his ear to ask, "Will that work? Did you miss me? Can I just stay?" He didn't put his arms around her because he knew he was weak for her and happy to have her back in his house and in his bed and in the kitchen between his legs and her mouth on his ear. He just needed to wait for Doris to leave and think clearly before making a decision, so he didn't respond to her.

Valerie said goodbye when Doris came back to the kitchen. Jefferson walked Doris to the car and they made plans to talk during the week about getting the appraisal for the house. She repeated to him, "Don't let your pride get in the way of a great love. You will never regret it, but you will regret it if you don't go for it."

He smiled at her and responded, "Thank you love counselor. Just be safe going home and call me when you get there." She quickly replied, "I will, and you better report that you are back together and the wedding plans are back on. Love you. Bye." She talked fast then rolled up the window, always having to have the last word. He laughed and waited for her to leave the driveway before heading back inside to talk with Valerie.

Valerie was waiting in the den. "Are you having Game Day today?" She needed to brace herself for what Jeannette might have to say. "No, Jeannette and Ann are out of town so it's just us today." Valerie smiled at hearing "just us today" and started getting excited. Jefferson, however, didn't have much else to say. He turned on the television and they watched in silence. During the commercial breaks, she asked questions to get caught up to his world.

"So Jeannette and Ann went away together? How is Ann enjoying her new place?"

"Yes, they went to New Orleans. Ann is good. Happy in her new life."

"And how is your business? Everything okay there too? How's Ron?"

"All good too." He was not going to make it easy for her.

Valerie asked whether he thought Steven and Nikki might finally date. She knew Nikki and Steven had talked and agreed to see what happened with Valerie and Jefferson before deciding how they should proceed.

Jefferson shrugged and said he had no idea. "When he finds out that you are here, we will see what they decide to do." Valerie noticed that he didn't say that Steven would find out that they were back together, only that she was at Jefferson's house. She tried not to take it as a sign of anything, just a choice of words.

He barely looked at her all evening and didn't touch her, not even when they went to bed. It was another restless night for them both. At around four in the morning, Jefferson eased out of bed again, this time going to the family room. Valerie went to the room a few minutes later and sat in the chair across from him.

"You are not sleeping. Is it because I am here? Do you want me to go?" She spoke softly. She didn't want to leave, but if this was not working they might as well cut their losses now.

"No, you don't need to leave. I need to tell you something. I want us to spend time together again, but I'm not interested in talking about marriage. I don't know if that means we will never get married or if it means that one day we will. I just want to move forward and see what happens. I know that I love you, I have missed you, and I'm glad you're here. That's all I can give right now."

"Okay. Me too."

Valerie then mentioned Lillian and Max's 35th anniversary party to see if Jefferson would still want to go. He said yes. It was in two weeks so Valerie hoped that she could spend the time with him even if she didn't move any clothes back to his house. She could go home during the day and change and pack for a couple of days at a time until he said he was ready for her to come back completely.

She went to the bedroom and took the engagement ring off and the AmEx card he had given her for the wedding out of her wallet and put them in the nightstand drawer where he was sure to see them. She got back in bed, anxious to see how he acted on Monday, whether he asked her to stay or come back after work.

When Valerie walked into the kitchen the next morning, Jefferson was at his usual spot at the table, looking at his worksheet. He looked up at her and said, "Good morning," but did not open his arms to greet her, nor did he ask if she wanted breakfast. She decided to see if she could come back to his house after work and asked what he wanted for dinner. He knew what she was really asking so he looked at her and tilted his head to the side, trying to decide what to say. "I'll bring something. I'll meet you here at six."

Monday night they had a quiet dinner and went to the den for the evening to watch television and read. He still didn't have much to say to her so she decided to give him some space. After they started watching a show, she went to the family room and sat quietly looking out the window until it was time for bed. She laid on him in bed, but he still didn't put his arm around her. The good news was he stayed in bed for the night.

When she walked out of the den on Tuesday after dinner and didn't come back for twenty minutes, he went to the family room. "Why are you sitting in here every night? I thought you wanted us to be together?"

"I do." Valerie's voice was clear and strong. "Except we aren't really talking or being together. I think you are still deciding if you want me so I am giving you space to make up your mind. I'm trying not to be overbearing or smothering."

Jefferson was annoyed. "If I didn't want you here I would not have gone out to the car for you. Or have you come back each night. Maybe it's you who is really trying to decide now that you have been back a couple of days."

"No, I'm very sure that I want you. I want us. I'm being patient and prayerful that you still want me. And us." She went back into the den with him and though the evening was quiet, there was less tension.

Valerie ended up staying the rest of the week, and their evenings slowly improved. They sat close on the sofa and he put his hand on her leg or draped his arm across the sofa and on her shoulder as they talked. He said a few more words to her each day.

Chapter Forty

The month of August brought Lillian and Max's 35th anniversary party. Both Jefferson and Valerie were excited to go. Jefferson saw it as a good break for them and maybe they could get close again, like they were before Vincent's accident. She was excited to see and celebrate her friends, still unsure of where she and Jefferson were headed.

Jefferson told Jeannette he was cancelling another Game Day and going to Austin for a couple of days to get away. He didn't mention going with anyone so she was hoping he was alone, or at least not with Valerie.

It was a black tie affair, their first together, so they spent time carefully packing for the weekend. They decided to go up on Thursday after Valerie left the flower shop so they could have time to tour Austin together, and so that Jefferson might have a little time to get to know Max before the party on Saturday.

When Jefferson and Valerie arrived on Thursday evening, they drove around Austin, noting all of the music clubs and restaurants, then checked into their hotel. Jefferson was still hesitant to get into their usual sleeping position so they slept side-by-side, holding hands and touching legs and feet.

They met Lillian and Max for lunch on Friday. Lillian and Valerie hugged and Lillian whispered, "See I knew you would be together. And you're almost married. I'm glad you took the chance." Valerie said she was glad too, except for the Mason family setback. Lillian was curious and decided to ask, "Do you want to be in the Mason family again?" Valerie admitted, "I really don't, but I know I've crossed a line or two, convincing myself I was doing it for Nikki's sake. The truth is I got caught up in those old family moments and regret it deeply."

Lillian watched Jefferson as he and Max got to know each other and before the afternoon ended told Valerie that Jefferson seemed more serious, solemn even versus the carefree way he was when they first had lunch at *Maggiano's*. She asked Valerie how they would get past the break-up and Valerie said she didn't know. Just time together she was hoping.

On Saturday, Valerie got dressed in the bathroom. When she came out, Jefferson stood up from putting on his shoes and whistled. She looked stunning in a floor length sleeveless silver lamé form fitted dress. The front draped softly just over her breasts and the back was open, the drape resting on the top of her butt. Her hair was pulled up in a twist that she and Stephanie had practiced when Stephanie was in Houston, making her neck and back look long and perfect for licking and kissing.

He looked like a model for GQ Magazine in a black tux with a black shirt and black tie. The look in their eyes confirmed that they lusted for one another and they said at the same time, "Party. Time to go to the party." The smiles on their faces were promises of things to come.

At the party, Jefferson noticed several men eyeing Valerie and finding their way to her to talk. She had visited Lillian and Max for a number of years so she knew a lot of their friends and both sides of their families. They were all happy to see her and wanted to catch up with what was going on with her and Nikki. Some were even happy to hear that she was divorced, thinking that she might now be available. Jefferson was sure that a couple of the men were flirting by the way Valerie gave them surprised looks or shook her head no at them. Instead of being jealous, he was proud. She was beautiful and handled herself well in social situations.

He was not without his own share of attention. While Valerie moved around the room saying hello to people, Jefferson sat at their table talking to their tablemates, or stood at the bar drinking a beer, meeting several of the men there. Most of the unattached women found their way to his side to engage him and offer their time for the evening and/or phone number for future conversations. He was relaxed and enjoying himself, flattered by the attention and polite but firm in saying no.

Valerie was watching him too. Just as dinner started, she walked over and kissed him in the mouth before they sat down to let everyone know, who didn't see them come in together, that he was hers. He smiled at her boldness, happy that she was giving him some attention. She whispered, "I love you." He looked in her eyes and responded solemnly with a nod, "I can see that. So can everybody else. I'm good with it. I love you too."

Throughout the evening, Jefferson and Valerie sat close together with Jefferson's arm across the back of her chair. They whispered in each other's ear. He was complimenting her on how beautiful she looked and how he was enjoying the night out with her. She told him how proud she was to be with him and that she missed being with him too. She put her hand on his thigh, looked seductively in his eyes and asked if Jimbo missed her. He promised her she would find out when they got back to their room. They both smiled at the thought of being together again. The anniversary festivities finally came to an end, and they wasted no time saying good bye.

Their night ended on a high note, both moaning for each other when their bodies were hot and sweaty, he could not get any further inside her, and passion consumed them. It was the first time they had made love since they got back together. It sounded ridiculous, even to him, but he needed to make love to her in a different bed than the one in his house to be sure that she called for him and no one else in the heat of passion. Then he would try making love at home in their bed again.

Chapter Forty-One

When Jefferson and Valerie got back to Houston, Nikki asked Valerie to come over to visit with her at her dad's house. She missed her mom, especially being so close in proximity. She wanted them to talk and hang out. Vincent was moving around with crutches and in a wheelchair so Nikki didn't have to be on call quite as much. Jefferson was a little wary, wondering what Vincent would have to say to Valerie and whether Victor would be there but Jefferson had end of the month business meetings and a major kitchen renovation for one of his houses so Valerie went alone. She went for lunch when Vincent was busy with therapy so she and Nikki could eat without him and have private time to talk.

Valerie shared details about the anniversary party. Nikki volunteered an update on her and Steven, now that she and Daddy J were back together. Valerie did not want to pry so she had not asked but was eager to hear the news.

"We are talking a lot and he and Jason have come out for a couple of visits. I told him that I was seeing Daniel back at home so we are still taking things slow. The chemistry is still there and still strong though." Valerie was happy with the fact that they were taking things slow. She had not met Daniel, but Nikki had been seeing him for a few months, so she wanted Nikki to be kind to him and not hurt his feelings.

Vincent asked Valerie if they could talk before she left. She was curious, especially to see what Jefferson had said to him that made him sign the divorce papers.

"Thank you for coming to the hospital to see about me." His eyes reflected his appreciation, a sincerity that she had not seen in a while. "It was good to wake up and see you. I know you were there for Nikki, but I am grateful nonetheless."

Valerie nodded her acceptance of his comments then said, "We had a few great years and you are Nikki's father. Someone needed to be there with you until your family arrived. I hope you changed your medical directive."

It was his turn to nod yes. Then he said, "I got the bike to help me loosen up and try something out of my comfort zone. Trying new things that you might appreciate as a sign that I was a more fun and engaging man."

Valerie did not respond, just looked at him to gauge his sincerity. Was he being nice and apologetic because he wanted the comfort she provided for him as family--a wife and mother, especially now that he had been hurt? On the other hand, was he for real, finally coming to terms with his life and his mistakes?

He noted her silence then continued. "You look great and you seem happy. Is that guy Jefferson giving you what you want? What you need?"

She smiled and said a firm, "Yes."

"So are you really going to marry him? You haven't known him that long, not even a year yet from what I understand. We dated for two years!" Vincent raised his voice. He was indignant.

Valerie gave him the slow, knowing smile of a woman in love and said, "Some things don't need a lot of time." She didn't want to say anything about planning to get married since Jefferson was not ready to talk about that yet.

Vincent gave her a long look and his final plea. "I love you Valerie. And I always will. I know we are divorced now, but if you ever want to try again, let me know." Then "daddy" Vincent spoke: "By the way, that Steven and his son, Jason? How are they connected to Jefferson?"

"His nephews. Why?"

"I think our little girl is falling in love. They talk every night and she is smiling every day. They came over on Saturday and Sunday the last two week-ends and stayed all day both days."

Valerie wanted his perspective. "What did you think of him, both as a man and a potential husband for her?"

"I like him actually. He was very respectful and attentive to her and to me. He took care of some things around the house that I was going to ask Stan and Richard to do. He said his uncle is an engineer and taught him about carpentry and building and repairing things as he was growing up, which is why he became an engineer too. He even cut my hair and shaved me. Seems to be a good father based on the way he talks with his son.

"And I didn't feel like he was sneaking around trying to get too personal or inappropriate with Nikki. They act as if they have been together a long time, moving around the house like they are at home, already married. Even Nikki and the little boy have bonded. He's always playing with Checkers, but he stays in the kitchen with her when she's cooking. Or she is reading to him. I hear them talking up a storm. Am I going to lose both of you to that family?" He looked sad.

"Nikki will always be your baby girl Vincent. Just get well so they can have some time to figure out what they are going to do before she leaves town." Valerie was glad to hear Vincent's take on Steven. At the end of the day, Vincent was a good father and wanted the best for his only child.

When Valerie got home, Jefferson was in the den watching the news. He looked at Valerie intensely then asked, "Hey. How was your day?" His tone was casual, but she knew him well enough to know he was anxious to know what happened between her and Vincent, even more so than with Nikki, but he would not ask directly.

She walked over to the sofa, kicked her shoes off and climbed up, straddling him to sit in his lap. They were face to face. She kissed him and smiled. "My day was great. I enjoyed Nikki and Checkers, had a good conversation with Vincent, and missed you. Did you miss me today or were you too busy?"

"I'm never too busy to miss you." He kissed her and rubbed her back and legs but was still looking for more information.

"Nikki says "Hello Daddy J," and Vincent thinks Steven is a good young man and that Nikki might be falling in love with him."

Jefferson nodded and smiled, but was still waiting to hear the rest of the Vincent story. "And?" He knew there was more.

"And he says you'd better stay on your game and take good care of me because he will always be waiting in the wings to take me back."

"It's a smart man who knows his place. In the wings. I'll always be on my game with you so no worries." Jefferson visibly relaxed and pulled her closer to rub her back some more.

For the first time since Vincent's accident, Valerie and Jefferson held each other in Jefferson's bed, feeling warmth and a certain hunger flowing between them again. He kissed her in the mouth for a long time, enjoying her tongue movements and what it felt like to breathe her breath.

His next move made Valerie lie still but be soft, willing, accepting. Jefferson proceeded to gently bite and then lick and kiss all over her body—shoulders, arms, hands, breasts, stomach, thighs, legs, between her legs in that place he enjoyed so much. He even turned her over so that he could bite and lick and kiss his way from her feet to her legs to her butt to her back and neck. It felt feral, like a wild animal was marking his territory.

She knew the bites were his expression of hurt, and the licking and kisses were to soothe the wounds—hers and his. When he turned her over onto her back again, she opened her arms and legs to him and Jimbo went to his happy place. Jefferson growled and pushed hard into her. She raised up to meet him. They moved together, making up for lost time, reconnecting, restoring, and renewing. Jeff was the only name that came out of her mouth and he noticed, rubbing her arms and hands in appreciation and holding her close in their favorite position when they fell asleep.

Jefferson prepared a bubble bath for Valerie to soak in the tub while he went to the family meeting and ran some errands on Saturday. He knew the bite marks were tender and the warm water would be healing. He came back late in the afternoon with a beautiful bouquet of Calla Lilies surrounded by Hydrangeas, and a bag of her favorite assortment of Ghirardelli Chocolates.

Valerie became hopeful that Jefferson was starting to feel that they were once again on solid ground, he would let her move back in, and they would start moving toward marriage again. She finally felt some of Jefferson's energy and excitement about them being together return. She started to feel the kind of love that she saw in Lillian and Max from the beginning of their relationship and through the years.

He realized he wanted to take another step with her. He still wasn't sure about the marriage, but he knew that he wanted them committed again.

Chapter Forty-Two

Steven was happy to hear that his uncle and Nikki's mom were getting back together. He asked Nikki for a date for the next weekend if she could get someone to sit with her dad. Nikki checked with her Aunt Viveca who couldn't come that weekend so Stan and Richard agreed to hang out with him. She knew her dad would be in good hands and she could relax and have fun.

Steven and Nikki started out early Saturday afternoon. Steven picked up lunch at *Katz Deli* then drove them to Hermann Park to picnic, people watch, and enjoy each other's company.

He had already told her his life story on their phone calls so he wanted to use the day to show her where he worked, where his mom lived and worked, the location of Ann's new house, and Jason's school.

Jason was with Carla's family for the week. They always made it a point to keep him for a week a couple of times a year in addition to days they would come over to visit with him or take him places for a few hours. It was a perfect time for Steven to show Nikki who he was, including where and how he lived since she had never been to his house before. He wanted to show her that she could trust him with her heart, starting with showing her his lifestyle and that he was not hiding anything.

He had a four bedroom flat with a big family room and kitchen. He gave her a quick tour, showing her his bedroom, Jason's bedroom and playroom, which took up two of the bedrooms, and the new guest room, Ann's old room. They sat in the kitchen to eat ice cream.

While they were talking, her phone kept ringing so she acknowledged that she was somewhat popular. She would check caller id then send the calls to voicemail so she could continue talking. Her phone rang again, she frowned when she saw caller id, then apologized. "I'm sorry for all the calls. I don't want to turn the phone off in case my dad needs me. There was a picnic today and people are looking for me. They don't know that I am still here."

Steven made a suggestion: "Why don't you answer the calls? Go into the guest room for privacy. We have all evening to talk. I don't mind."

Her phone rang again. Steven got up. "I'm going to clean up these dishes. Go take your call. Then we will watch a movie and talk some more."

He pulled her up from the island and gently pushed her toward the guest room. While he cleaned up the dishes, he thought about their conversation and decided he was getting too old to play games. He had a son watching him so he had to do the right thing. He wanted her, from the day they met until today. Being honest was necessary so if she was not interested, they could agree to be friends and move on. It was a gamble. He would find out tonight if it worked.

Nikki took the call and it was Daniel, upset that she had not answered his calls and not understanding why not since she was with family. "Or are you with family?" he asked. Nikki knew he sensed another man around her. He would question her about other men even before she met Steven, which made her hesitate to commit to a relationship with him. She thought he might be too jealous. They talked for a few minutes and hung up when she promised to call him the next day.

When she went back to the kitchen, Steven was popping popcorn and pouring them some wine. He took his usual direct approach to ask her about Daniel. "Was that him? Is that why you didn't want to answer?" He needed to know if there was serious competition from someone else who had captured her attention and what he might have to do to get her to focus on him.

She was quiet for a moment, and then admitted, "He's getting a little anxious with me being away for so long. Before I left, he had suggested that we be in a committed relationship. I have not agreed yet."

"Yet?" Steven repeated.

"Well, he wants it to be."

"And you? Do you want to be serious with him?" Steven pressed. He needed to know what, or more accurately who, he was up against. A long distance relationship was hard enough without some local competition in the mix.

Nikki did not respond right away, spending a minute looking at Steven with her head turned to the side. "I don't know yet. Tell me what you are looking for."

"To be honest, until I saw you that day, I wasn't looking for anything or anyone. Work and Jason and Saturday family business meetings and Sunday Game Day filled my life. I hang out with my friends every now and then, but I haven't dated since Carla died even though I'm around women all the time and some even ask me out. I have always said no thanks.

"But you Ms. Mason, you make me want to change things up. To be totally transparent, and this is not something I should admit right now since we are just getting to know each other, but when I saw you that day at Unc's house, I knew immediately I wanted to spend a lot of time with you, and probably get married sooner rather than later."

"Really? Just on site? Married?" She questioned him even though she had the same feeling herself. "How do you know that our seeing each other wasn't just a wake-up call for you to start dating again? Dating other people until you find the next Mrs. Jackson? Saying yes to some of the women you previously said no to?"

"How do I know? Because since that day I have not thought of anyone but you. I still don't want to date anyone else, and every move I have made over the last few weeks, especially getting Ann out of the house and on her way, was to prepare to see you again and see if my gut, my heart, are telling me the right things, that you are the one I want.

"Here is another truth that men don't normally admit in this kind of situation, so early in getting to know someone: I dated a lot in my past life. Dated all kinds of women—older, younger, Black, non-black, rich, poor, middle class. It was fun and kept me busy. But I knew the day I met Carla that those days were over. And after five years of being alone, raising my son and not dating, I have that same feeling again. For you."

"So Nikki, here we are. What are you thinking? Would you consider us having a long distance relationship?"

"I want to, but between the distance, my mom and Daddy J not quite back together, and your mom doesn't like my mom and probably not me, and you have a child, a son…it's a lot."

Steven paused before responding. "Yes, it's a lot. But is it too much for you, for us to handle together?"

Nikki did not comment right away, spending a few minutes looking at Steven. He decided not to push her to verbalize what she was not saying in her silence. It may have been more that Steven wanted to hear right now. Instead, he invited her to the family room to watch a movie, taking the popcorn and wine. They sat on the sofa together, choosing the movie *Brown Sugar*, something they both had seen before and could talk through as the movie progressed. Only neither one was paying attention to the movie.

Chapter Forty-Three

In her mind, Nikki was comparing Steven and Daniel. They were both educated, rising to success in their industries, considerate, fun men. Steven was sexier and definitely better looking. There was no drama with Daniel. He was single and had no kids. And he was close by so they could date every week, which they had been doing until she came to Houston to be with her dad. She liked that, knowing she had someone to go out with on a regular basis. It had been a long time since she had dated anyone special, but she was not quite sure that Daniel really was special, given his suspicious nature. After being with Steven, she was definitely having second thoughts about Daniel.

Steven decided not to press Nikki to want to be with him. She was right, there was a lot going on around him. He knew his time for dating was limited so he respected her desire for a more traditional relationship. However, he was not above satisfying his curiosity and giving her something to think about.

He put his glass and the popcorn bowl down then leaned over and took her glass out of her hand, pausing for just a moment to look into her dreamy eyes before taking her head in his hands and leaning in for a kiss. It was his first in five years so he was hesitant, timid at first. She tasted like the sweet wine and smelled like fresh peaches. His senses were on overload so the kiss became more intense. Tongues were moving in and out of each other's mouths, his hands left her face and his arms wrapped around her, pulling her to him as he leaned back on the sofa. Her body pressed into his and her arms wrapped around his neck.

The moaning started in her throat first, then moved into her mouth. The passion moved from her into his mouth and he started making his own sounds and talking to her. "You smell good. You taste good. This is really good to me." His lips moved to her cheeks then her neck and up to her ears and back to her mouth. She was ready for him to kiss her some more, then she went in search of her own taste of him, lightly licking his neck and ear lobes and rubbing his chest and back. It got hot very quickly and it felt good to them both.

Steven finally stopped kissing Nikki and turned around to give her back her wine glass and pick up his wine to cool off. She was leaning back on the couch watching him, believing that he was being considerate of her relationship so she didn't say anything. They both faced the television, licking their lips.

But it was too late. The fire the kiss started raged out of control. They both put their glasses down and turned to each other at the same time. Lips locked and clothes started coming off. She didn't have on much, a short dress with a bra and panties.

She had taken her shoes off at the door. His shirt and jeans and underwear left a trail to the bedroom. Climbing into his king size bed gave her goose bumps all over and she shivered in anticipation. He rolled on a condom out of the box that he bought as soon as he got her number. He started talking and declared with a smile, "It's been a while so this could last a minute or all night." Nikki smiled back and said, "I'm good either way." She did not want him to feel pressured.

Steven leaned in to kiss and caress her body. It had been so long for him he didn't want to rush. He wanted to feel her soft skin and smell her arms and hands and legs as he went searching for the happy places that made her moan. He was so gentle and tender that when he slid inside her, her breath caught in her throat. She felt like he was worshipping her, body and soul.

It lasted much longer than a minute, but not all night. She could take all that he gave and let out a hissing sound then a long 'y-e-s-s-s' when he hit just the right spot. He came with her. After the second time, they were drenched in sweat and took a shower, changed the linen, and finished the wine and popcorn. Both were quiet, not questioning what was next or making promises that they would not keep.

He took her back to her dad's but before she got out of his car, he asked for her travel plans. "When are you heading back to Chicago?"

"This is my last week of FMLA," was her quick reply.

Perfect, Steven thought. "Okay. Do you think you could get someone to sit with your dad the rest of this week in the evening? Since Jason is with his grandparents until next Sunday, how about we spend my free time after work together? I'll pick you up when I get off work and we'll explore Houston together. You show me your favorite spots and I'll show you mine."

Nikki didn't miss the double entendre and was happy to say yes. They made plans for the next night at 6:30p.m.

He smiled all the way back home, sure that he had given her something to make her believe that the issues she listed earlier could be addressed if they were together. Only time would tell if she got the message he was trying to convey.

Nikki was glad her dad was asleep when she got in. She thanked Stan and Richard and asked them if they could come back the rest of the week in the evening. She would cook them dinner in return. They said yes, and instead of each one taking a day, they decided to come together.

She went right to bed, wanting to think about Steven uninterrupted as she replayed the evening in her head. He was smart, fun, and funny just like she thought he would be, plus a good storyteller, and very caring about her feelings and her situation. One thing was for sure: she never felt so good, from head to toe.

On the other hand, Daniel was pressing for a commitment. She had been putting him off while her dad was in the hospital, but now that he had been home a few weeks, she was running out of excuses. She told Daniel the next day that she was heading home on Sunday so they would talk then. He reluctantly said okay which left her free to enjoy Steven.

Nikki and Steven were together every night that week. Dinner, bowling, roller skating, miniature golf. Yet somehow they always ended up back at his place. Steven had been quite the player before he met Carla, even dating older women who taught him how to thoroughly love a woman's body then practicing on quite a few young ladies his own age. He used several of the techniques he learned with his tongue and his hands, making sure every part of her felt his touch. He was sure Nikki would remember him for a long time, and hopefully, realize that they belonged together.

On Friday, Viveca came for the weekend and Victor was coming back on Sunday to stay with Vincent for the next two weeks while Nikki went home.

Nikki spent the weekend with Steven. It was their last two nights together before Jason came home and she headed back to Chicago. They had a sensual and sexual marathon all over his house so they each would have good memories while they were apart. They went to sleep exhausted both nights and spooning, not wanting to be far away from each other. On Sunday, their last morning together, he woke her up early for one last experience and he realized that she had been imprinting her feminine wiles on him too. He was already missing her being around his house as well as in his bed. She was smart, fun, and very sexy. It was going to be interesting to see if Daniel stayed around much longer. He decided to let Nikki contact him if she was interested in having a relationship.

Daniel met her at the airport with flowers and a big hug. She knew immediately and without any doubts that Steven was the man she wanted. The conversation in the car on the way to her apartment ended with Daniel being moved to the friend zone. He didn't seem to be as upset as Nikki expected and she was glad. She did not want any hurt feelings and hoped that he had found someone else while she was away.

She waited a week to call Steven, taking the time to be very sure that she wanted him, Jason, Jeannette, and to move back to Houston sooner rather than later if his interest in marriage was real. There would be no turning back once they were in touch again.

He was in bed for the night after getting Jason settled in his room and his clothes ready for school when his phone rang. Her name on caller ID made him sit up on the side of the bed. He waited to hear some good news before getting excited.

"Hey Nikki."

"Hi Steven. Is this a bad time? Is Jason in bed?" She was a bit nervous.

"It's a perfect time. Jason is sound asleep. How are you?" He wanted her to lead the conversation.

"I'm good. Been busy getting back into work projects."

"I understand that. You were away for quite a while. Checkers back into his routine too?"

"Yes. I think he missed being here but he keeps looking at the door, like someone should be coming in. It's hard for him to settle back down to our quiet little life after being around so many people every day."

"So how is Daniel?" He decided he couldn't wait.

"He is good." She paused then continued. "We decided to just be friends." She wondered how Steven would respond. The ball was now in his court.

"Are you okay with that? You were considering a serious relationship with him when you were here."

"I'm fine with it. It was my decision." She was happy to give that report.

"Okay. Well let me ask you the question you never answered at my house. What about the possibilities of us? Is my life, my son, my mom, your mom, and my uncle…too much or are you ready to give us a shot?"

Nikki paused for a long time before answering. "I'm ready. Ready for all of that."

"Are you sure? A readymade family? My very formidable mother Jeannette Jackson? And we need to stay together no matter what happens between Unc and your mom." Steven asked, shaking his head. "It's still a lot. You need to be sure."

"I'm sure," Nikki exhaled. "Very sure." She wanted the roller coaster ride with Steven, Jason, and Jeannette. A big, messy, loving family. She also wanted to be close to her mom again, and Daddy J.

"But what about you? Do you still want this long distance relationship on top of what you already have going on?"

"I've wanted you since the day I met you. The distance is just a factor to deal with for now. I have not changed my mind."

"Okay. So now what? How do we do this? A long distance relationship is all new to me." She was definitely excited now.

"It's new to me too. Let's hang up so I can video call you. I need to see that pretty face and watch your sexy lips tell me you want me." He was excited.

They agreed to nightly video calls after Jason was in bed and they agreed to be together again the very next weekend. By that time, they would have been apart for two weeks. Nikki had a work project to finish on Saturday so she and Checkers would come back to Houston on Sunday and stay until Tuesday. While she was in town, they would figure out the schedule for the rest of the year.

Chapter Forty-Four

Jefferson had Valerie park in the garage for Game Day so that space in the driveway would be left for Jeannette as usual. Jefferson's truck took up the other spot in the driveway. Steven always parked on the street.

The minute Jeannette walked in the door and saw Valerie the war started. They were in the kitchen and Valerie was laying out utensils and plates for the food. She stopped when Jeannette screamed at Jefferson.

"What is she doing back here? Are you two together again? Getting married? How could you be so stupid? She already broke your heart once. How many more times do you need her to do that before you learn your lesson?"

Jefferson looked at his sister with the 'Ware stare' and asked her, "Are you done? Because this is my house and if you don't like who is here, feel free to go to your own house, or wherever else you want to go. I will not be talked to like I am a child, nor will you disrespect Valerie in my home. Make up your mind before you say another word."

Jeannette went to the den fuming. She would wait for Steven before deciding if she was going to stay.

The door buzzed and opened to Steven, Jason, Nikki, and Checkers. Steven and Jason had picked up Nikki and Checkers from the airport.

Nikki greeted Jefferson in the family room as if she had not just seen him two weeks before. "Hey Daddy J. Long time…Did you miss me and Checkers?"

"Of course," he replied with a big grin on his face. "Your mother is in the kitchen."

"Good, cause I need to hug my mama." She headed for the kitchen and they gave each other hugs. Valerie gave Nikki the heads up, "Jeannette's not happy. We had better walk softly."

When Checkers ran into the den, Jeannette went ballistic. Saying in a loud voice to no one in particular, "And she's here too? Oh my God. Where is Deuce? Does he know she's here? He was doing just fine without her. Are we back to this messy circle again?"

Nikki, Steven, and Jason walked in the den and Steven said, "Yes mom, we are here. All of us." Nikki and Steven looked at each other like they did on the first day but Jeannette stopped their starry eyed gaze at each other. "Deuce? Deuce? Look at me. Did you know that she was coming today? Are you two dating now? What the hell is going on?"

Steven was smiling at Nikki as he responded to his mother. "Yes in fact, we are dating. What are you so angry about?" His mother's outburst was unusual.

VALENTINE LOVE

"I just wish someone had warned me that the love fest was back on again. I would have stayed home. In fact, I'm going now. I don't want to watch Jeff get hurt again and probably you too."

"What makes you think we will get hurt?" Steven was frowning at his mother. "Why are you all riled up about our business? You have never done this before."

"Let's just say I have good intuition. I'm out." She never spoke to Valerie or Nikki but stopped to hug and kiss Jason. He was busy playing with the dog and that pissed Jeannette off too. She stormed out and slammed the door.

Jefferson was the first to speak. "I'll be right back." He loved his sister and didn't want her to leave so angry although he didn't want her in his or Steven's business. He caught her at the car. "Jeannette you have got to calm down and understand that we are going to do what we want to do with these women. Are you still angry about the property? Valerie and I have not talked about that in a while."

"I am still concerned about the property, but I'm more worried about you. You went into a funk for weeks, acting like you were ok but hiding behind fixing Ann's house like a madman or hibernating at home. I didn't know what to do to help you so I was just glad you and Valerie broke up and hoped that she didn't come back. I don't like to see you hurt. You are my rock. For me and Deuce and Jason. If you are not strong, the rest of us have no one to lean on. I'm afraid our family will fall apart. On top of that, Deuce wants the daughter. Who knows what will happen there. I can't handle you both being in a mess. Spare me the drama."

Jefferson shook his head, shocked at her admission. Then he offered, "Or you can embrace the women in our lives and be happy that we are happy, for whatever time we have with them. If it turns out that we will not be with them, let us wrestle with that. I appreciate your love and support. But this rage of yours is ridiculous." He headed back to the house. Jeannette sat in her car for about five minutes, debating on whether to go back in. She drove away.

Chapter Forty-Five

"Welcome back to Game Day," Jefferson said facetiously to Valerie and Nikki when he came back to the kitchen. No one commented on the previous outburst by Jeannette. Instead, they all grabbed plates of food and headed for the den. Before dessert, Nikki and Steven went to the family room to talk without Jason listening.

"How about this--let's see if Uncle Jeff and Ms. Valerie will watch Jason for a couple of hours so we can go figure out our lives together." Nikki was happy to agree.

When they walked into the den, they were holding hands. Jefferson and Valerie both looked up at Steven and Nikki, saw the grin on their faces, and knew that they were happy. Valerie was happy for her daughter and for Steven.

Jefferson and Steven shared a look, a man-to-man, "I got my woman" look and nodded at one another.

"We need a favor." Steven was looking at Valerie and then Jefferson.

"Yes, we will keep them. Have a good night." Valerie and Jefferson said the same thing at the same time then smiled at each other, glad to be in harmony.

"Good night? No, no. That's not what I meant. Jason has school tomorrow. We will be back around 7 so I can get him home and to bed." Steven was not asking for all night. He took care of his son and tried not to push him off on other people.

"It looks like you two need to talk and spend some time together. Just be here early with his clothes and book bag to pick him up." Jefferson understood that Steven needed more than a couple of hours. He had been waiting for Nikki for a long time. But Jefferson was not sure that Valerie was okay with her daughter spending the night out with a man so he looked at her for confirmation.

Valerie smiled with a tinge of sadness, looking at Nikki. "My baby has been a grown woman on her own for a long time. Take care of her Steven. See you in the morning."

Steven and Nikki both went over to hug Jefferson and Valerie, then said goodnight to Jason together. Jason promised to watch Checkers and get his bath and go to sleep on time, especially if Checkers could sleep with him. They all said yes. Steven and Nikki left, anticipating a very fun, good night together.

Jefferson put Jason and Checkers to bed and found Valerie in the kitchen cleaning up the last of the dishes. She stopped when he came into the room to ask, "Do you think I should try to talk to her? Jeannette?"

"To say what?" Jefferson knew that Jeannette was being sincerely concerned but still unreasonable in how she expressed her anxieties. "She will not be satisfied unless you tell her that you are leaving me for good and she can relax. Is that what you want to say to her?" He gave Val a look that said speak now if this isn't working for you.

"No, that's definitely not what I had in mind. I want you and I'm not going anywhere again. I just thought it was time we got to know each other, just the two of us. Maybe then she can feel less threatened and less protective of you. Plus I don't want her to be nasty toward Nikki either. Maybe the three of us need to have lunch together sometime too, when Nikki has time."

"Might not be a bad idea. I'll talk to her about it and if she agrees, find out when she would be available. Thanks V. I appreciate your concern for her in spite of her crappy attitude."

To Jefferson, it was nice that he didn't have to deal with Jeannette on his own, that Valerie saw an opportunity to bond with Jeannette. That's what true partners do, help each other navigate life and relationships, especially family.

To Valerie, it would be her opportunity to say to Jeannette, "I'm not going anywhere so get used to the Mason women. We are not bad people, and who knows, you might actually get to like us." She was even more excited to hear Jefferson call her V again instead of Valerie or Val. He was slowly warming back up to her and talking in a loving way.

Chapter Forty-Six

While the relationship between Valerie and Jefferson was on a slow crawl, Nikki and Steven wanted to go full throttle now that they were on the same page about wanting to be together.

When they went to Steven's house, they made love then pulled out a calendar to schedule visits and calls. They decided that Nikki would come to Houston every other weekend right after work on Fridays, and Steven would fly to Chicago, sometimes with and sometimes without Jason, as often as he could in between her visits. Video calls would happen every night so they could see each other and share their day's events.

The first order of business would be to introduce Nikki to Jason as the girlfriend, not just Checkers mom and Ms. Valerie's daughter, and make sure Jason was comfortable with that.

Steven was already thinking about sleeping arrangements during her visits. Nikki had plenty of places to stay in Houston. Steven wanted Nikki to stay at his house when she visited but he also had to set a good example for Jason so he wasn't sure how to make that happen.

The sleeping arrangements when they were in Chicago would be awkward. Nikki had a one bedroom apartment and a king size bed. With so little time to spend together in a weekend, they did not want Steven and Jason to stay in a hotel unless they all went together. They both laughed when Nikki said, "I have a feeling we will all be in my bed together, with Jason and Checkers in the middle." Steven gave her a quiet smile and said, "Welcome to parenthood." Nikki gave him a big smile and said, "I'm good with it. Jason is a good kid, polite, smart, and fun. He has been growing on me since we first spent time together. The bigger question is how he will feel about me being around your home instead of Ann. And what about Ann? How will we work on that so she is okay with us actually being together now?"

"Funny you should mention Ann. She is already dating so I have a feeling she will be okay with it. I'll talk to her before Jason makes an announcement to her though." Steven knew he had better call Ann on Monday to be sure.

Since it was almost October, they also thought about Thanksgiving and Christmas. Nikki always came home for both holidays anyway so nothing would change. Christmas definitely had to be in Houston so that Jason could be home with his toys and gifts. Nikki would schedule time in Houston from Christmas through New Year's Eve.

Steven voiced his concern when looking at the calendar. "This is a lot of travel on you. I'll pay for your tickets, but are you sure you want to spend so much time in the air?"

Nikki was clear and decisive in her response. "I know its harder for you to travel, with or without Jason, so I'm good with it for now. Let's see how it goes the rest of the year then we can re-evaluate things."

The next morning when they went back to Jefferson's house, Jason was up with Checkers. Jefferson had made him breakfast and fed Checkers when Steven and Nikki walked in. Steven went into daddy mode, asking about his night, if he had fun, and did Checkers sleep with him. Jason was just as curious. "Were you and Ms. Nikki out together? Where did you go?"

Steven and Nikki exchanged a look and dived in. Steven explained, "Yes, we were out together. We were talking about her being my girlfriend. What do you think of that? Would you be okay if she and Checkers stayed with us at our house sometimes? And we could visit her and Checkers in Chicago too."

Jason looked at his dad and then at Nikki, a little confused. "So would you be my girlfriend too?" Steven laughed and said, "No man. We can't have the same girlfriend. One day you will have your own. But a long time from now."

"So will Ms. Nikki sleep with you like Ms. Valerie sleeps with Uncle Jeff?" That question took everyone by surprise. The things that kids notice.

Steven decided to take advantage of the opening and said, "Yes, at our house when she visits."

"So if you are daddy's girlfriend, what will you be to me? Will you be my godmommy?" Jason only had one frame of reference for women in his dad's life.

Nikki responded gently. "No honey. Ms. Ann is your godmommy and she is so special that you don't need another one. I'll still be Ms. Nikki while we get to know each other better. Will that work for you?"

"Okay." Jason went back to eating and Steven reminded him to hurry so he could get to school.

When Steven and Jason were leaving, Steven gave Nikki a hug and a quick peck on the lips goodbye in front of Jason to see how he would react. Jason had not seen his dad kiss a woman like that so he asked why he did that. "Because that's what girlfriends and boyfriends do. They kiss hello and goodbye, sometimes on the lips."

Nikki asked Jason, "May I give you a hug and kiss too? I will kiss you on your cheek if it's alright with your dad."

Jason wanted to be like his dad so he looked at his dad for confirmation that he could get a hug and kiss. Steven cautioned him, "Only from Ms. Nikki because she is special. Don't give your hugs and kisses away to just any woman."

Nikki leaned over and Jason reached up for their first hug and kiss. Jason ran out the door telling his dad he got a hug and kiss too! Steven winked and smiled at Nikki and waved to Jefferson and Valerie. He was already having a better day than he had had in months. He was very happy and looking forward to many more days of happiness with Nikki and Jason.

Chapter Forty-Seven

The relationship between Steven and Nikki was off to a good start. Jason was on board with his dad having a girlfriend. Steven called Ann to tell her that he and Nikki were officially dating. She seemed genuinely happy for him. She had found a special guy too so there were no hard feelings. He made it a point to remind her that she was always welcome to Game Day on Sunday's and asked her to feel free to bring her friend too. She was family and he wanted her to always be included in their functions. She thanked him for saying that and said maybe one day. "Let's see what happens with you and Nikki. I don't want there to be any issues with Jason thinking he has to choose between her and me." Steven shared his appreciation of her for that and hung up with a happy look on his face.

While Steven was talking to Ann on Monday, Jefferson got Jeannette to agree to lunch with Valerie so they scheduled it for Saturday after the family meeting. The meeting that Valerie still wasn't invited back to. Surprisingly Valerie was not bothered by that since it was still such a sore spot with Jeannette.

Valerie and Jeannette met at *Tony's Italian Restaurant,* a popular upscale restaurant that was a favorite for both of them. It was white tablecloth classy and a quiet atmosphere, perfect for their conversation. They were two very beautiful women so they were interrupted a couple of times by interested suitors but since they were each in relationships, they said, "No thanks," to the men who stopped by the table or offered to buy them a drink.

After they ordered drinks, salads, and entrees. Valerie started the conversation. "Thanks for suggesting this place. See, we are already off to a good start since we both love Italian food. Plus we are both mothers with great only children, and we both love Jefferson. I can't be all bad, can I?" She was trying to start light before digging in to the property conversation. Jeannette was quiet and watchful, waiting for Valerie to reveal her true intentions.

"Okay, let's just cut to the chase, talk about what you call "the elephant in the room." The property. I understand your concerns. I would probably have them too if I were in your place. Here's the deal: I am proud of all that Jefferson has accumulated and like the way he has the business set up. I have nothing to contribute to that more than the comments I've made and questions I've asked at the Saturday meetings, based on owning property when I was married, my background in math, and accounting classes I've taken. I am most excited about the fact that he is successful *and* has time for a relationship, which my ex-husband, Vincent, rarely chose to make time for in his rise to power—at least not with me. He did with a younger woman that worked with him which is why we are divorced. Thankfully, his ambition and success paid off financially so I got a nice divorce settlement. I can take care of myself. Very well."

They paused the conversation when their drinks came and then their salads and finally their entrees. Jeannette remained quiet, looking around the restaurant while Valerie looked at Jeannette and thought about what to say next. When they finished eating, Valerie continued the conversation.

"I told Jefferson early in our relationship that I am not interested in the property, but he is a man's man and wants to take care of his woman. Or should I say his wife because outside of you, he would not take care of just any woman. He said he would work it out and you and I would learn to live with whatever he decided so I have not mentioned it and he hasn't either, especially since our recent split. And I won't mention it now since I'm barely back with him and just able to visit the house." Valerie gave her the "girl I am not crazy" look. Even Jeannette had to smile at that.

"All I'm saying is I want us to be friends, and maybe one day sisters if Jefferson ever really forgives me and we get married. And I want you to get to know and care about Nikki as a niece." She paused then said, "Maybe even a daughter-in-law at the rate Steven and Nikki are going. Nikki will get everything her dad has amassed financially so she will never need the property either. How about this…truce? Friends? Or at least friendly?" She held out her hand.

Jeannette looked at Valerie's hand for a long time before she reached out to take it. Instead of shaking it immediately she held it in her hand and said, "My brother, my son, and my grandson mean everything to me. I want us all to be able to enjoy the fruit of our labor. Mine and Jefferson's. It's hard to share. Let's start with friendly." With that, she smiled and shook Valerie's hand.

Jeannette continued to talk. "Thank you for asking for this time together. I can be a bit possessive when it comes to my family, and hard to reason with. I am not ashamed of that. I actually think you are good for my brother even though I was ready on a couple of occasions to find you and kill you for hurting him. I believe he still loves you but after Alicia, I'm not sure how forgiving he is willing to be. So be patient. I will not try to influence him one way or another." She gave Valerie the 'Ware stare' and they both laughed.

Jefferson had given Valerie a credit card to pay the bill so once that was taken care of they stood to leave. Jeannette gave Valerie a hug. "Go get your man girl. I'll be watching and waiting."

With that, they got into their cars and drove away. Jeannette immediately called Jefferson and pretended to be mad that she had to suffer through lunch with "that woman." Then she laughed and said she was good with Valerie and wished them well. When she asked if he and Valerie were getting married, Jefferson was non-committal. "Mind your business," was all he said to that. "And thank you. I love you sis."

When Valerie got back to Jefferson's house, he was in the den in his favorite position, legs outstretched on the coffee table, waiting for her report of the lunch conversation. She laid across his lap and laid her face in the crook of his neck. She put his arms around her and hers around him.

"I think we made some headway. She promised to give me a chance. The question now is do I still have a real chance with you?"

"That's why you are here," he commented, rubbing her arm and kissing her forehead.

"But you haven't said I could move back in. Nor have we talked about getting married." Jefferson did not respond and stopped rubbing on her and kissing her. She raised up to look in his eyes but he leaned back and closed them. She decided to let it go for now and give him another month. If there was still no progress to marriage, she would figure out whether dating would be enough for her or if she should go home and not come back.

It was his turn to want the plain ole tight body soul satisfying straight up missionary sex that she had asked for after her bath. He used it to try to communicate that he still cared very much and he was doing the best he could. She knew what he wanted, needed actually, and was happy to provide it. This was one night they skipped dinner and focused on dessert. She took that as a positive sign.

Chapter Forty-Eight

October turned to November and Nikki and Checkers came back for their next visit. Steven and Jason picked them up from the airport and they went directly to Steven's house, spending the evening together as a family. They cooked burgers and fries, and Nikki taught Jason how to play an old card game called Pity Pat. He only needed to match two of the same cards so it was easy for him to learn and he had fun.

As it got dark, Jason asked his dad if Ms. Nikki and Checkers were going to spend the night. Steven said yes because they were boyfriend and girlfriend, then asked him if it would be okay, because if not, he would take her to her mom's condo or to Uncle Jeff's. To an adult it was clearly a set-up. Steven and Nikki knew Jason was having fun and enjoying the family time so he said yes, it was okay.

They brought Nikki's bags in and put them in Steven's room. Jason watched but never said a word until his dad was making sure he got his bath. "So are we sleeping in your bed tonight?" Steven said, "Yes, but just for tonight. Then you and Checkers will sleep in your room." Jason nodded okay, happy that Checkers would be sleeping in his room with him.

When Steven and Nikki were ready for bed, he moved Jason and Checkers to Jason's room. The next morning, Nikki asked Jason to help cook breakfast for his dad so he was happy, never mentioning that he woke up in his own bed. Every night thereafter, Jason went to sleep in his own bed with Checkers in his room. That was the start of their new arrangement when Nikki came to town.

Nikki visited with her mom on Saturday while Jefferson and Steven and Jason were at the family meeting. They went to the *Buy Black Marketplace* at the *Shrine of the Black Madonna Cultural and Events Center* to shop and have lunch, then joined the guys for dinner at six. Both Valerie and Nikki liked that they would see each other more often and could hang out together.

In between Nikki's visits, Valerie still stayed at Jefferson's house but only night and casual clothes were left in the closet and drawer. This way, she had something to sleep in and something to put on in the mornings to go home to change if she was going out. He still had not given her the garage door opener back. He would always open the door so she could pull her car in at night. Valerie started to feel like he was punishing her. Or signaling that he was not going to let things go back to the way they were. She began to realize that she just might be the "lady he's dating," and would not end up as his fiancé again and probably not get married.

Lillian and Valerie had been talking after the anniversary party but Valerie never told her how she had messed up the relationship. Lillian pressed Valerie for a wedding date, reminding Valerie that

Jefferson had said they would be married before the year was out. Valerie finally had to confess to the fact that there had been a major change in their relationship and why, and that she was beginning to conclude that there never would be a wedding. Lillian was disappointed for Valerie because she knew how much she loved Jefferson.

Lillian came to Houston for a visit two weeks before Thanksgiving. She asked if they could all have lunch at *Maggiano's* again on Saturday. She wanted to see for herself whether things had changed that dramatically between Valerie and Jefferson. Valerie hosted Lillian at her condo instead of Jefferson's house so they could talk. Lillian could see the sadness in her friend.

When they got to lunch, Jefferson asked Lillian to catch him up on Max and all the people he had met at their party. He kept the conversation going with current events and other general topics. She could tell that Jefferson was quiet and more distant with Valerie, not playful and fun as their first lunch had been. Her heart broke for her friend.

That night, Valerie told Lillian of her plan to give Jefferson until Christmas to decide about their relationship and if they had not at least talked about marriage by then she would stop staying over with him and see if she could get someone else to love her. Lillian understood and agreed with her plan.

Thanksgiving came and Nikki was back. Dinner was always at Jeannette's but they all could cook so they each brought a dish or two so it would not be a burden on Jeannette. Jeannette's friend Ed came so he met the family for the first time. Steven and Jefferson asked her and Ed all kinds of questions about when they met, what he did, where the relationship was headed. Jeannette was embarrassed and told them to "mind their own business." Jefferson and Steven both laughed and said to her, "Oh yeah, right. Sounds familiar doesn't it?" All of the women laughed at the irony too.

For the rest of the weekend, Valerie and Jefferson went shopping for Christmas gifts on Black Friday and Saturday, then hosted Game Day on Sunday. Still no word from Jefferson on their relationship so when the games were over she packed up to leave when everybody else left. Jefferson asked her where she was going.

"I need to take care of some business early tomorrow before I go to work so I'm going to go home tonight to be able to get dressed and leave easily from my place." Jefferson was immediately suspicious but didn't say anything. When she didn't come back Monday night after he got home from work he was sure that something was up with her. He called and she was sleeping at 7pm.

"What's going on Valerie? Why aren't you here? And why are you asleep so early? What happened today that you are so tired?"

"Nothing's going on. It was a long day so I decided to just stay here instead of packing up and driving over to your place. I didn't realize how tired I was when I came in or I would have called to let you know before I fell asleep. I'm sorry."

"So are you coming over tomorrow?" He could feel that she was blowing him off.

"I need to wash clothes and clean my apartment. You are welcome to stop by if you are out and about. I can come over Wednesday if you're going to be home."

Jefferson knew this was a turning point for Valerie. She had grown tired of waiting for him but would not push him. He could feel a brush-off a mile away. "Alright then. Dream of us." He hung up and spent the next two hours pondering her moves. Valerie was not stupid nor was she a manipulator so she was not playing games. He had some decisions to make.

Chapter Forty-Nine

The next two weeks leading up to Christmas followed the same pattern. She slept at her condo and stopped by his place during the week when he was home but always left because of early meetings or things to do the next day. She used Christmas shopping or preparation for Christmas as her excuse.

On Friday's she packed to stay at his place for the weekend. They rode around to look at the Christmas decorations one night, and went to the holiday party hosted by Zeke and his wife the next night where she met some of his other Air Force friends. They wrapped the gifts for the family together one evening, and had fun laughing at stories Jefferson told about some of his friends that she had met.

Christmas Eve was a cool weather day so Jefferson started a fire in the fireplace and they drank eggnog and listened to Christmas music, telling each other stories of Christmases past when they were growing up or as adults.

He went to the kitchen to get dinner started and laid the garage door opener and a new security card and code at the place where she usually sat.

When she walked into the kitchen, they were the first things she noticed. She sat down and looked at them then him. Neither of them said a word. She left them on the table the whole evening, trying to decide if she should take them at face value, as a sign that they were just taking a step forward or if they needed to talk about whether she could also move back in. He noticed that she was not as enthusiastic about getting them back as he had hoped.

Christmas morning they woke up early and made love but it felt different. Valerie had a sense of foreboding, as if it would be their only Christmas together even though he was offering the garage door opener and door code. Jefferson was concerned that she would not accept the gifts he had for her. They opened their gifts in bed.

Valerie had purchased a special watch that Jefferson had his eye on and she had it engraved 'There's always time for us. V.'

He first gave her a double row Marquise diamond bracelet in 18k white gold, which she loved. He held his breath as she opened the second box. It was the engagement ring that she had left in the drawer a couple months earlier. He had wrapped it in a big box. When she opened it, the shock on her face told him he was right, she didn't think he wanted to marry her anymore and that's why she was pulling away.

"I never stopped loving you V. But it's been difficult for me to trust you again. I told you that was an issue for me when we first got together. It has taken a minute for me to let my love for you and your love for me, replace my trust issues. But love rules, love wins for me for us. I hope it still does with you."

She was looking at him with tears standing in her eyes. She waited to compose herself, clearing her throat and wiping her eyes. "It does, even though I had lost hope." Valerie whispered.

"I know. I could tell. And I'm sorry it took me so long. Here's the thing though. I still want us to get married before the end of the year, preferably on New Year's Eve. Just us and whoever is here that can make it. I know it sounds crazy since I'm the one who has been dragging my feet, but I want us to start the new year married and you moved back in here. Will that be okay with you? And lunch afterwards. We will decide on a place for a honeymoon and go on Valentine's weekend. Fay will just have to do without you helping out at the counter this time around. Please?"

"Yes, we can do that. I love you so much Jeff. I'm glad we can get past the past and that we didn't completely lose our way. Thank you."

He then showed her the wedding bands that had arrived that week to confirm that he was indeed serious and ready to get married right away. She rolled over into his arms and squeezed him tight and they held each other for the next ten minutes before getting dressed for the day.

Family Christmas brunch was at Steven's so everyone could see what Santa had brought Jason and exchange gifts with each other. Jefferson and Valerie were both quiet and happy that Jason was the center of attention so they didn't have to say much.

They didn't want their news to overshadow what was happening with Jason and all the gift giving. Jeannette, Ed, Ann and her friend Phillip, Vincent, and Carla's parents were there.

The big surprise was when Steven and Jason proposed to Nikki. Their conversations had started about the fact that the end of the year was at hand and they needed to plan their new schedule for visits, but they had not talked about marriage. Steven had received blessings from Nikki's mom and dad, Uncle Jeff, and his mother so he hoped that Nikki would say yes.

Nikki opened the last of her gifts while she and Steven were on the floor playing with Jason and Checkers. When she saw the ring, she looked up and Steven and Jason were both on one knee, saying simultaneously, "Will you marry us?" She looked around at everyone like time had stood still, watching their expressions. Each person she looked at was smiling and nodding yes. Her eyes landed on her mom and Valerie winked at her. Then she looked at Jason and finally Steven. Steven held her hand and said solemnly, "I love you. We love you. Please say yes."

Nikki said yes and burst into tears. Steven and Jason both hugged her and each kissed one of her cheeks. Steven put the ring on her finger. Nikki kissed him again then jumped up to hug her mom whose eyes were filled with joy, happy for her daughter.

Jeannette poured champagne for everyone and the conversation started about when Nikki would move back to Houston and when the wedding would be.

Jeannette was the first to notice the ring on Valerie's hand. "What do we have here? Are you two engaged again?" Her voice got everyone's attention.

Valerie and Jefferson answered together, smiling. "Yes, we are." Valerie explained why they didn't say anything earlier. "We didn't want to spoil the night for Steven and Nikki. We might as well tell you the rest: we are getting married on New Year's Eve and you are all invited. We will be working out the details in the next couple of days."

Shouts of congratulations rang out and Jefferson pulled Valerie into his arms. He knew she was still feeling a bit surprised and he wanted to assure her that he was there for her. All in forever.

Nikki came over to give her mother another hug. They were happy for each other. She hit Jefferson in the arm and said playfully, "It's about time. I was getting scared that you were going to flake out on her." He responded honestly. "I was a little slow but here we are."

The celebration for both couples continued for another half hour then everyone started to leave. Valerie and Jefferson went back to Jefferson's house and they spent the rest of the evening in their favorite position for sleep but not sleeping. They wanted only to hold each other, feeling a renewed sense of peace allowing them to cleave to one another.

Chapter Fifty

The day after Christmas the wedding countdown began. The biggest items on the list were finding a chapel that was available on New Year's Eve, and securing reservations at a restaurant for lunch. Since Valerie had already been getting information from churches and her favorite restaurants, she called them back to see which ones had space for them on New Year's Eve and made reservations.

Nikki called and asked if she and her "husband and sons" could come over for a few minutes after lunch. They wanted to talk to them about something. Of course, Valerie said yes. When they arrived, Steven and Nikki were glowing with happiness and Jason was calling Nikki "Momma Nikki," and Checkers his little brother.

When they were all seated in the den Nikki asked them for a favor. Jefferson and Valerie each assumed it was a request to babysit and were about to say "of course" when Nikki continued. "Steven and I would like to get married with you on New Year's Eve. A mother and daughter double wedding. Would you mind? Would you be okay with that?"

Valerie and Jefferson were stunned into silence. They looked at each other and back to Nikki and Steven. Valerie was floored, and began firing questions. "What? Why? What about a big wedding for you Nikki? You've never been married before. Don't you want that? I don't want you to miss out. Have you talked to your dad about this? I think he has held visions of walking you down the aisle for a long time. And I know he's got money set aside for your wedding." Valerie didn't want Vincent to feel left out. This was his only child.

When Valerie finally took a breath, Nikki responded. "The simple truth is we don't want to wait. That big wedding stuff is ridiculous and expensive. We have a family already and I need to go back to Chicago and quit my job and pack to move and look for another job. I want to get back here to live within the next thirty days. Or less. Nobody has time for a big wedding. We have a life to live.

"I'll talk to my dad. He can come to Chicago and help me pack and we can drive back together and do some more father/daughter bonding. And he can save my wedding money for his grandchild."

Valerie and Jefferson were startled to hear her say that. They looked from Nikki to Steven to Nikki and said together, "Are you pregnant?"

Steven and Nikki laughed and she said, "I knew that would get your attention. No, we are not. But we might want to start sooner rather than later, while Jason's still young but can be the cool big brother. I told you the day I met Steven and ruined

Game Day that I wanted to have his baby. I still feel that way and he is looking forward to adding another Jackson to the world at some point. So what do you say? Can we have a double wedding? Please mom? Daddy J?"

Jefferson asked Steven, "Have you talked to your mother about this?"

Steven was happy to report that Jeannette Renae Ware Jackson was perfectly fine as long as she could be a part of the planning with Nikki and Valerie. "Nikki has said yes. What say you Auntie Val? Or may I call you Momma Val?"

"Auntie Val? Momma Val? Don't try to butter me up." She had a big grin on her face when she said it. "Give us a minute and we will get back to you." Valerie and Jefferson went to their bedroom to talk.

"Surprise, surprise. What do you think Jeff?"

He repeated what he had said all along. "It's your day. Have whatever wedding you want. Just tell me when, where, what to wear. I love Steven and Nikki so whatever we can do for them is fine with me. But first I want you to be happy."

Valerie thought for a moment then nodded yes, happy to be able to share this day with her daughter.

When they went back to the den, Valerie and Jefferson had somber, poker faces. Steven and Nikki looked at them, then each other, and back at them.

"We would be honored to get married with you! Yes, let's do it." Valerie and Nikki hugged each other and did a happy dance. Steven and Jefferson said they needed a drink because they could see already that it was going to be a long week. They were smiling at each other when they said it.

Valerie called Fay to tell her about the quickly approaching wedding and the need to take the week off. Fay was thrilled for her cousin and happy to inform the staff of their invite to the festivities on New Year's Eve.

The first order of business for the two couples was getting the marriage licenses so that they met the 72 hour minimum wait period before the ceremony. They all went to City Hall as soon as the office opened the next business day.

The men were assigned the task of moving Valerie back into Jefferson's house before the week was up. She was happy to finally be packing all of her belongings for the last time.

Valerie, Jeannette, and Nikki dubbed themselves "The Trinity" and wasted no time in getting together to plan events of the wedding day while helping Valerie pack. Valerie even asked Jeannette if Ed was ready to pop the question and they could do a triple wedding. Jeannette gave a resounding "No," so they continued the planning for two couples.

Jeannette was thrilled to be hanging out with Valerie and Nikki and being a part of the activities. She was looking forward to the three of them being family, in and out of each other's homes and lives.

Vincent came by Jefferson's to ask if he could pay for everything, including all of their dresses and tuxes, the photographer/videographer, the church, the luncheon, limousines, and honeymoon suites for both couples on the night of the wedding. He said he had budgeted for a much larger wedding for his daughter so the money was already there. He needed to do something special for his Nikki, and he wanted to give Valerie a great send-off to her new life.

He explained to Valerie and Jefferson it was his apology to them for causing trouble by delaying the divorce. "I was doing what men do—trying to get the great love of my life back. I had to learn that I was not and am not Valerie's great love. Apparently you are. So my plan backfired. I want to show you my appreciation for your kindness to Nikki and give a final goodbye to the life I had with Valerie." Jefferson thought it was unnecessary but Nikki asked him to say yes. Valerie was happy to spend more of his money. Vincent gave Nikki a credit card to use for all of the expenses.

Since Valerie had found the church and restaurant on such short notice, the women visited each place to decide upon flowers and other decorations and the menu. Then they went dress and shoe shopping. Nikki and Valerie both wanted something they could wear again, definitely not the traditional long white wedding dress for Nikki. Jeannette got a new dress too as mother and sister of the grooms.

There was a bit of a chill in the air on the morning of New Year's Eve, but the sun was shining. The brides and grooms were ready. Limousines picked up the ladies at Jeff and Valerie's house and the men at Stevens. When they arrived at the church, their favorite family and friends were there to witness the commitment to one another and to lifelong love. The Mason's were there: Vincent, Victor, and Viveca;

plus Stephanie; Fay and her husband and staff; Lillian and Max; Stan and Richard and their wives; Carla's parents; Ann; and Doris.

Vincent walked Nikki down the aisle to Steven and Jason. Max did the honors to get Valerie down the aisle to Jefferson. The minister was known for very loving wedding ceremonies that even made the most confirmed single people want to say, "I do." He was especially good on this day, and happy to do it for two couples at one time. That was a first for him.

Lunch after the wedding was beautiful and festive and Jeannette and Vincent were the perfect hosts. Vincent spared no expense in picking up the tab, including a three-day stay in a penthouse suite for both couples at separate five star hotels, with champagne and flowers placed in both suites. The limos came back to the restaurant to drop them off at their hotels, and would pick them up again when they were ready to return home.

When midnight came, Steven and Veronica (Nikki) Jackson, and Jefferson and Valerie (V) Ware, were watching the fireworks out of their respective hotel windows and happily making plans for their new lives.

# # #

ABOUT THE AUTHOR

PAM KELLY spent her teen years on Chicago's South Side reading romance novels and watching her parents live out their own real life love story. After earning two masters degrees and having a successful career in advertising, she went from studying brands to studying the magic and nuance of relationships – her own and others – and now writes about them in sensual romance novels. Her characters are bold and strong, flawed and sensitive, and all kinds of sexy. Their stories are compelling, heart wrenching, and romantic.

Pam loves reading, music, decorating, a good laugh, and beautiful shoes. Her goddaughters and nieces and their children keep her busy and up-to-date on all things new. She resides in Houston, Texas.

Connect with Pam online at PamelaFKelly.com

www.ingramcontent.com/pod-product-compliance
Lightning Source LLC
Chambersburg PA
CBHW051937290426
44110CB00015B/2011